A COWGIRL'S BOOK OF MEMORIES

by Gale C. Ginn
1923 -

This is NOT a book of fiction. The events described here are real; the
settings and characters are intended to represent specific places
and living or deceased people.

All illustrations/photos provided by Author.

All rights reserved. No part of this manuscript may be reproduced

Or utilized in any form or by any means, chemical,
electronic, inter-dimensional or mechanical, including photocopying, recording or by any
information storage and retrieval system, without
permission in writing from the author or her heirs.

Inquiries should be addressed to:

Gale C. Ginn
421 Doña Aña School Road
Las Cruces, New Mexico 88007

Order this book online at www.trafford.com
or email orders@trafford.com

Most Trafford titles are also available at major online book retailers.

Printed in Victoria, BC, Canada.

ISBN: 978-1-4269-1791-2

*Our mission is to efficiently provide the world's finest, most comprehensive book publishing
service, enabling every author to experience success. To find out how to publish your book, your
way, and have it available worldwide, visit us online at www.trafford.com*

Trafford rev. 12/28/09

 www.trafford.com

North America & international
toll-free: 1 888 232 4444 (USA & Canada)
phone: 250 383 6864 ♦ fax: 812 355 4082

DEDICATION

This one is for my family,
friends, and all those men
and women who gathered,
branded, punched cattle
or raised hell in Arizona
Circa: 1900-2008

ACKNOWLEDGEMENTS

I DON'T BELIEVE ANY BOOK, much less mine, could be written without the help of writers, editors, family and friends and the like.

So I would like to thank and acknowledge the following people who have been such a wonderful help to me with this book. They are: Pam Kochery, David and Cathy Rockwell, Donald and Betty Minden, Ann and Michael Stewart.

I've given it my best for an Old Broken up Cowgal. I hope I've pleased you with the results.

Sincerely, Gale C. Ginn

INTRODUCTION

ALTHOUGH THIS BOOK OF stories began back in the 19th Century, I started accumulating memories about them during the early 20th Century. These stories have served me well throughout my life. Some are good, others—well, I'd just as well forget a few of them, some are funny or sad, some I still hold close to my heart. Family and old friends have requested I put them down on paper so other folks can enjoy them too. I hope you enjoy them as much as I did living most of them . . .

HISTORY

There was one special day in the passage of time

That will bring a smile when brought to my mind.

I wanted God to freeze it and let it go on.

It was too perfect to think it would ever be gone.

There was so much history packed into the room,

That the stories and memories started to bloom.

We stayed in our chairs but we did take a walk,

Down memory lane, as we turned back the clock.

With memories sharp, Aunt Gale would begin

Then after she got it started Dad would jump in.

They told of things, long since turned to dust.

Of cowboys and drinking and rounders that cussed.

About things that were funny and things that were sad.

Times filled with blessings and times that were bad.

They told of rustlers with their six guns shinning bright.

Of getting back stolen cattle by standing to fight.

Trouble and work didn't scare them. They wouldn't think to

run.

They sucked it up and did what ever needed to be done.

Their stories about a family of hardy women and men.

And I'll bet if you asked them, they would do it all again.

I know the ones a telling it, wouldn't trade the life they've had.

Because the memories still make them smile, the good out weighs the bad.

It's because of them and what they did, that we are who we are.

And I would bet that those who've gone have roped a shooting star.

Questions were asked and Poems were recited.

Happiness reigned and all were delighted.

They made us all wish we could go back in time.

And savor the presence of those who've left us behind.

We'd be sure to capture their essence and remember all they said.

Take in every detail and weave it in our memory with strong thread.

That day friendships were formed and family discovered

Memories relived, and things forgotten recovered.

I shall cherish more, the ones that they tell me today

Because these days that are special shall too pass away.

This poem was by my niece Linda Hartlieb

Story Index

Page   Story Title

Page	Story Title
1	The Beginning—1860'S
5	Sod House
35	13 Year Old Gale's 312 Mile Ride
41	Gale's Ride
47	Life Beyond High School
52	Gale working in the movies
54	Gale's Movie Stories
63	Grandmother mary
66	Introduction to short stories
67	Mable Rathbun-Conroy
71	aunt mable
76	Dale's Stories
81	Marvin 'Cheyanne' Chamberlain
85	Tommy conroy
89	The Ranch
94	Story Of The Round Elevated Tank
97	The Runaway Wagon
98	Nora And Tom
100	Some Of Grandmother's Medical Recipes
102	Grandmother And Sammy
103	Aunt Mabel At The Ocean
105	The Sooty Stovepipe
106	Queen Elizabeth

107	Mother And The Biscuits
108	Clayton And The Secret Box
109	Smokey And Dale
110	Tommy's Times At Cochise
111	Mother, The Paint Bucket And The Ladder
112	The Old Square Grand Piano
114	Ditch Day
115	Buck 'Crashed' Our Hen Party
117	Cloverdale Picnic
119	Grandmas Almost Boyfriend
120	The missing body
122	Pecos Higgins
124	The Story of Calico
130	Calico's Poem
134	MY Dear Irish Queen
135	My Name is Pecos Higgins
137	Barney
139	Hell On The Mountain
141	How I Growed Up
142	Prison
144	I Dreamed I Was Riding A Pony
146	Ghost City
148	Desert Dusk
150	The End
151	Glossary of western terms

PHOTO INDEX

Page	Photo Title
14	Family Tree
15	Grandfather Charles Rathbun
16	Grandmother Mary Rathbun
20	Front-Midwife Permit
21	Back-Midwife Permit
23	Orchestra w/Mabel & Bernice
23	Model-Bernice Age 20
24	Model-Bernice in 1908
24	The Rathbun Home in Kansas
25	Stave Mill w/Grandfather Charles
26	Bernice & her cow
27	Photo of Pearce, AZ w/ cowboys in 1914
28	Bernice's Tent house 1911
30	Hauling Water to the homestead
31	Adobe House w/ Baywindow
33	Photo of Bernice & Pecos on honeymoon ride
35	Dale's first paying job
52	Gale's ride Part 1
53	Gale's ride Part 2
54	Gale's Ride Part 3
55	Newspaper letter about Gale's Ride
56	Follow up letter about the ride
63	Branded Movie Poster
64	Untamed Frontier Movie Poster
65	Photo of Wranglers used on Branded Movie

72   Mural on side of feed store by Gale
73   Gale reciting a poem for Wellspring Church
79   Grandmother Mabel's Rock Fireplace
80   Bathtub mural
84   Bernice & Mabel
87   Photo Of Brother Dale-1976
89   Dale Roping a deer
90   Two photos of Dale's roped deer
92   Chy on horseback
100   The Old Ranch House
102   `Aerial view of the Ranch
105   The Elevated tank
108   Tom & Nora Stafford
130   Gale, Pecos and CGee
131   Calico
138   Pecos, age 72
139   Pecos & Buck discussing the finer points of booze
152   Gale reciting a poem at the Cowboy Picnic

THE FAMILY TREE

Updated: 12-8-2009

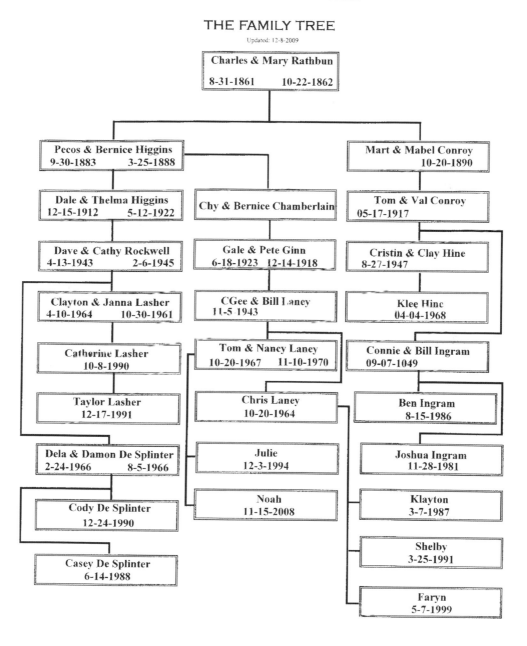

Charles & Mary Rathbun
8-31-1861   10-22-1862

Pecos & Bernice Higgins
9-30-1883   3-25-1888

Mart & Mabel Conroy
10-20-1890

Dale & Thelma Higgins
12-15-1912   5-12-1922

Chy & Bernice Chamberlain

Tom & Val Conroy
05-17-1917

Dave & Cathy Rockwell
4-13-1943   2-6-1945

Gale & Pete Ginn
6-18-1923   12-14-1918

Cristin & Clay Hine
8-27-1947

Clayton & Janna Lasher
4-10-1964   10-30-1961

CGee & Bill Laney
11-5 1943

Klee Hine
04-04-1968

Catherine Lasher
10-8-1990

Tom & Nancy Laney
10-20-1967   11-10-1970

Connie & Bill Ingram
09-07-1049

Taylor Lasher
12-17-1991

Chris Laney
10-20-1964

Ben Ingram
8-15-1986

Dela & Damon De Splinter
2-24-1966   8-5-1966

Julie
12-3-1994

Joshua Ingram
11-28-1981

Cody De Splinter
12-24-1990

Noah
11-15-2008

Klayton
3-7-1987

Casey De Splinter
6-14-1988

Shelby
3-25-1991

Faryn
5-7-1999

Grandfather Charles Rathbun

His mother was of Pennsylvania Dutch extraction, and his father claimed an English and Powatan Indian heritage. He had grown up hunting, fishing, and swimming in the rivers in that area. His father owned a local sawmill, so his children had the advantage of going to school and led a truly a carefree life until the sawmill burned to the ground. After that, they decided to move West, since that seemed to be where the big opportunities were happening back in the 1800's.

They came from New York as far as Hutcheson, Kansas, and while there, the boys all found work so their journey was suspended for a short time.

Gale's grandmother, Mary Berkey, was born in Poke City, Iowa on October 22, 1862.

Grandmother Mary Rathbun

Mary was a vivacious, proud young woman. Grandmother Mary told Gale she remembered her trip from Iowa in a covered wagon when she was only five years old, and hearing the men hollering, "Circle the wagons, the Indians are coming."

Her grandmother's life had been a hard one because there were nine children when her father had brought them to Colorado in search of that ever elusive gold. During this time Mary's mother died leaving a six-month old baby to be cared for.

Mary was only 11 years old, when her brothers and sisters all ran away due to her father's strictness and cruel punishment for disobedience. Grandmother said she could never blame them for leaving, as he would hang the boys by their feet and whip them with a bullwhip. The sisters were old enough so that they could go into the dance halls and saloons of the mining camps as fast women. Even with all of this, Mary still stayed and took care of her baby brother and her father.

Her father finally gave up on the gold and moved to Kansas to file on a homestead, living for some time in a sod hut, as did many of their neighbors.

Sod House

FOR THOSE OF YOU folks from the late 20th & early 21st Century, you might find this interesting:

Sod House [SH] construction goes back to the days if the Vikings. Even the Eskimos used the basic principals to build their igloos. During the mid 1800s up to the early 1900s, immigrants to the mid-western states were forced to use this type of house construction because the plains didn't have many trees and therefore lumber was all but non-existent.

First, these settlers would look for grass with densely packed roots like Buffalo, blue stemmed or wheat grass. The plains states were covered with these grasses.

Second, they would take a tool called a breaking or grasshopper plow pulled by a horse, Oxen, and sometimes a cow. Using these plows, they would cut very long strips of sod one foot wide by four inches deep. Then using a knife, hatchet or axe, they would cut the sod into three foot long bricks. That gave them a brick of sod one foot x four inches x three feet.

The settlers would lay out the house footprint to take advantage of the sun, wind and weather as advised by the plains Indians. A typical SH was roughly ten feet by sixteen inside the sod walls.

Third, the settler would begin alternately stacking the sod lengthwise and crosswise with the grass side down. They would install the wooden door and window frames as the wall rose up. When the frames were encased in sod they would use long wooden pegs to fasten the frames to the sod. A wooden plank was usually installed over the window frame to keep the weight of the sod from breaking the window glass.

Fourth, the builder could select to build either a pitched roof or a slanted roof. Since lumber was pretty scarce in the early days, the builder would use saplings gathered from the nearest stream, creek or river—if any. Using what they could find, the builders would erect a ridge pole and using the saplings, they would weave a roof of sorts. They would then use more sod to cover the roof. Slanted roofs were constructed in the same manner.

When the first rains came, the SH roofs would spring leaks and leave muddy floors inside. You can imagine what the house wife thought of that. As time passed and small towns sprung up here and there, the settlers began to build their roofs using wood sheeting, tar paper covered with sod.

Now, that you've had a tiny glimpse into the past Grandmother Mary lived . . .

They homesteaded near Hutchison, Kansas, and here, Mary went to work under the watchful eye of a German doctor who thought she had great potential in medicine. He trained her to be a top-notch nurse and she was able to get her midwife's license. A mid-wives job was mostly birthing new babies. However, they also took care of folks down with the illnesses of the time.

Take the time to read the Midwife permit below. Kinda tells ya how things were done back then. You see, Doctors were far and few between in most rural areas of the United States. Mid-Wives were the forerunners of modern nurses.

- Setting broken bones

- Cleaning wounds *(including gunshots)* and burns
- Bathing patients, mothers-to-be, babies, etc.
- The list is endless . . .

It was not an easy task to find a Doctor out in the country. Most Doctors had an office in their homes in the towns throughout the Southwest. If you lived several miles from the nearest town it could take several hours or even days to fetch the Doctor and return to your spread. Roads? No, my dears, ours were just plain old dirt trails rutted by wagon wheels for the most part.

Midwives played and important role in survival back then. Most of them, like Mary, learned of several home remedies from the local Indian Medicine men.

When you read the back of their permits, it tells it like it was.

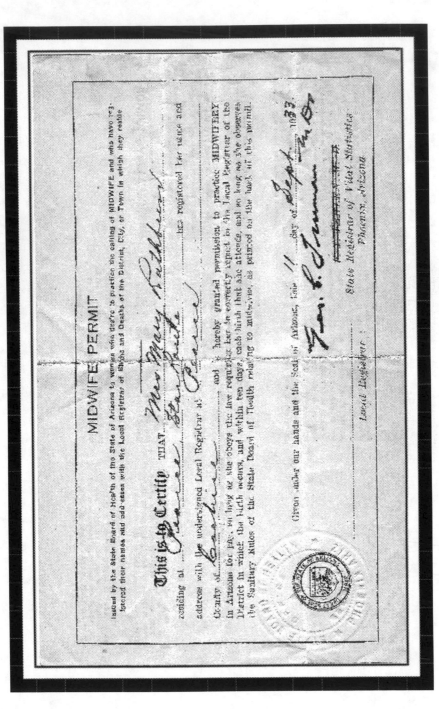

Midwife Permit - Front

MIDWIFE SAFETY RULES

Rule 1.—A midwife, before attending a woman in confinement, must wash her hands and arms with warm water and soap (preferably an approved antiseptic soap); and afterwards, if she has not used antiseptic soap, soak in a quart of warm water containing 2 teaspoonful of Lysol or bichloride of mercury.

Rule 2. She must keep herself clean and her face, head, clothing, and all that comes in contact with her.

Rule 3. She must not pass her fingers or any instrument into the birth canal of the woman, for the purpose of making an examination or for any other purpose.

Rule 4.—A midwife must endeavor to secure the assistance of a physician if the child is not born after twenty-four hours of labor.

Rule 5.—A midwife is not permitted to give drops of any kind to the mother before labor, but may give warm drinks or other liquids as needed.

Rule 6.—She must not give an injection of any kind into the birth canal without advice from a doctor (she may use an enema of warm water into the bowels to produce a movement).

Rule 7.—If the child's head comes down and the cord is being held, press needles and extract the born alone (send for a doctor at once, telling him what you have noticed).

Rule 8. If the child's feet or buttocks are born first, it will be awkward in a few minutes unless the head comes out feet first, but in such a case the midwife should lift it up first of the child by the feet and hold it up. This will scald the delivery at the head; failure to do this means certainly even the death of the child.

Rule 9.—If the mother has a sudden, or severe illness before or after the child is born, and it seems serious, she should send at once for a physician. Do the same thing if the mother's legs swell or her labor is slow. If the mother shows signs of fever, send for the physician at once and do all you can until she is seen. These unusual prcompts, she may do, do not rely upon yourself to carry a physical womans about the care must send for a physician as quickly as you can.

Rule 10.—Every midwife must make, in all cases must record the birth she attends well in ten days she can receive certified here. There is a fee for making a record (with the enclosing blank and receiving fund).

Rule 11.—To PREVENT SORE EYES AND BLINDNESS the midwife, or doctor should drop into the eyes of each child at soon as born, two drops of one per cent aqueous solution of silver nitrate. This drops will not hurt the baby's eyes but will prevent infection and possibly blindness.

BUREAU OF VITAL STATISTICS
STATE BOARD OF HEALTH
PHOENIX, ARIZONA

Midwife permit - back

9

While at a country dance, Mary met Grandfather. She had been called in to be the second on the organ for a new fiddler in town. Grandfather was straight, very handsome and was driving a good set of mules for his buggy. All the girls were flocking around him and Grandmother immediately set out to capture his heart— she always loved a challenge.

After they were married, Grandfather went to work in the salt mines nearby. Grandmother worked in a local laundry. These were busy years for them. First, Bernice was born, then Mabel 18 months later. After that, Grandmother decided they didn't have enough resources for more children and through her medical training they were able to limit the size of their family. They didn't have family planning back in those days . . .

Bernice was the outdoor type. She loved taking their milk cow out along the railroad tracks to graze. In those days, the trains were all coal burners and the coal carrying cars would lose a lot of coal alongside the tracks. Bernice would pick it up, put it in gunnysacks, tie the two sacks together and let the cow carry them home for her. Remember, in those days, a lot of people burned coal in their cook stoves.

Mabel was more social and loved to spend time with her friends, roller skating and going to parties. She loved dancing, and sharing things with her friends.

Both girls grew up musical and they played in an all girl orchestra around 1906. Bernice played the cello and Mabel the violin.

See photo next page

While in school, their teacher became interested in Bernice's artistic talent and began to encourage her along this line. However, even when Bernice was small, her Grandmother Rathbun taught her to embroider, crochet, and to sew. When Bernice left the 8th grade, she went into a dress making shop, and Mabel took a business course after the 8th grade and went into that field.

Mabel Bernice

At age 20, Bernice worked with a Photographer

Bernice as a photographer's model in her handmade dress. 1906

In 1909, this young Kansas lass, Bernice, turned 21 years old. During all of her years growing up, she had fanaticized about finding her 'prince charming' who she visualized as a wild cowboy. She would have a little cottage in the West, grow tomatoes, have a milk cow and, oh my yes, make her children mind.

The Rathbun's Kansas Home

During this time, the Arizona Territory had opened up for people to file on a homestead of 160 acres. A group of Kansas's people around Hutchison got together, and packed their few belongings when they discovered they could get a train to take them to their new destination in the Arizona Territory by rail. When Bernice Rathbun heard of this, she was quick to join the group. Then, the big job she had to face was going home and breaking the news to her folks, who of course had a lot of reservations about her being in a wild country alone.

Her father Charles decided he would go with her, although he was more of a city boy than a Western pioneer. He was working on a barrel

Stave Mill and after work there was always a lot of socializing at the local billiard hall.

Grandfather Rathbun 3ʳᵈ from left bottom

Bernice had become a seamstress after graduating from the eighth grade and had saved her meager salary toward filling her dreams. She bought a tent; a milk cow and a pitcher pump for her well. When they were ready to leave, she put the tent over the back of her milk cow and wrote 'Arizona Territory or Bust'.

Bernice and her Cow

The train stopped at a little mining town in the Arizona Territory named Pearce. They were met by land agents who took them into the country in horse drawn buggies where the land could be homesteaded.

Pearce was founded in the late 1880's as a major gold and silver mining community. The mining continued until ground water rose higher than they could pump it out. It was full of bars, brothels and frontier folks. Pearce was located in the famed Sulfur Springs Valley in south eastern Arizona, 75 miles from the Mexico vs. US border. Pearce was completely surrounded by US government homestead land.

Although the majority of the Kansas settlers picked out homesteads in the area called the Kansas Settlement, the Rathbuns picked out their homesteads to the east of the settlement in the Light area.

Pearce & Local Cowboys in 1914

Bernice chose a spot nestled down in the Sulpher Springs Valley about 12 miles East of Pearce. Her father filed on his homestead nearby. Bernice pitched her tent and soon realized she would have to dig out a depression to make enough room for her father to stand up as he was six foot tall. She told me they would move the table and chairs inside in the day time then out at night so they could bring in their bedrolls. The following photo was taken after she closed in the tent with wooden siding.

The enclosed tent house in approximately 1912
with Grandmother Mary holding Dale

Bernice said she soon found, that in this wild country, her pitcher pump was of little use because the water level was down approximately 80 feet and it couldn't draw water. She arranged for a neighbor to haul barrels of water to her from a spot called Seep Springs.

Unfortunately, she didn't have a horse or a buggy. There were so many things she was going to need, and she realized she was going to have to find some kind of work and since there was no market for a seamstress, she would try her luck at the nearby Chiricahua Cattle Company (CCC). So she donned her sunbonnet and started walking across the open prairie. When she arrived, she was met by Ike Deadman, the ranch foreman at the West Wells Ranch.

When she told him what she wanted to do he said, "Little girl, do you think you could cook for about 60 old grouchy cowboys?" She told him she surely would like the chance to try, so he hired her. The going wage was $30 a month at that time.

The first evening she was peeking around the door of the dining hall to see how her dinner was going over. She heard Ike Deadman say to the cowboys, "if you eat all the chuck *(sic-1)* you get to kiss the cook." Bernice rushed back to the kitchen and made another big batch of biscuits.

Pecos Higgins and a friend had heard the CCC was hiring a few cowboys. They were riding in that direction when they came upon a pretty little girl hoofing it across the prairie in her sun bonnet to go to work. Pecos stopped and said, "little girl where are you going?" she told him, so he said, "why don't you hop on behind my friends horse as mine won't ride double." Pecos had forgotten how ticklish Bill was when Bernice got on behind him, she put her arms around his waist to hang on. Bill was so ticklish he jumped and so did his horse, Bernice's feet went into the horse's flanks and almost got them bucked off.

This was Bernice's first meeting with Pecos Higgins, and although she didn't know it at the time, he was to become her 'prince charming'. Both Pecos and Bill hired on with the CCC. Pecos kept finding all kinds of excuses to go to the cookhouse to be near his little doll. One day, Pecos told Bernice there was a dance at the Roper Dance Hall about 18 miles from her home and he would bring her a gentle horse if she would go to the dance with him. Her father was reluctant to let her go with this wild cowboy but Bernice was headstrong and said she would be fine. True to his word, Pecos brought her a fine gentle horse for her to ride and off they went.

On one trip to the Roper's Dance she found all cowboys were not gentlemen like Pecos was. She was invited to another Roper's Dance with another cowboy who was definitely not a gentleman.

This feller let her know she was 10 miles from home and there was no one to help her and he was going to have his way with her.

This fast thinking little Kansas gal said, "OK, but get down and spread out your saddle blanket." While he was doing this she took her quirt and whipped his horse that jerked away and headed back for the ranch. The next day about noon this old kid came in carrying his saddle and blanket, and the foreman, Ike Deadman, told him to keep on walking, you're fired. He said he would not have any cowboy on the ranch that didn't respect a woman, especially their little girl cook.

At Grandpa's homestead, they discovered her pitcher pump wouldn't work there either, and so—they had to take turns digging a well. They hand dug down to about 80 feet to find water. To make do, they hauled water in barrels on a wagon pulled by one saddle horse because they had not been able to acquire a team. Bernice said money was scarce and she had to wait for necessary things.

Hauling Water

It wasn't long until Mary and Mable decided to join them. Bernice had learned how to make adobe. She made the forms and pretty soon she and Mable got busy playing with mud. Bernice was a builder and it wasn't long before they had a small adobe house ready for their parents. She even put in a bay window in the South wall for her mothers house plants.

The bay window is on the left

Then, it was time to get busy and build their own houses. Mable had filed a homestead adjoining her father's homestead. Bernice called her place 'Happy Hollow' and Mable named hers 'Hungry Hill'.

During this time both Bernice and Mable worked as cooks on neighboring ranches to supplement funds to get what was needed; like teams of horses, a buggy and a hand plow and a windmill and to add to their cowherd of two cows. Somehow they were sure that some friendly bull would find his way to keep their cows company.

Mable went to work for another ranch as a cook and the ranch was called the Double Rods which was the brand they used on the ranch's cattle. This ranch was owned by the Hood Family.

Mable was sort of a nanny, did the cooking and cleaning and the washing for the family. The going wage was $30 a month.

Mable worked for this family for over a year until a young wild cowboy, Mart Conroy, got her fired. She was washing the evening dishes and Mart was pretty drunked up. He had come to take her to a Ropers Dance and she told him she could not go until the dishes were done. He walked over, grabbed the dishpan, dumped water and dishes and all into the stove wood box. Sure enough they were a little irate and gave Mable her walking papers but good cooks were few and she had no problem finding another job.

Mart Conroy was a young man whose family had sent him to the military institute at Roswell, NM. After graduation he went to the Douglas, AZ area to be near his sister and brother in-law who had a big ranch in the southern part of Cochise County. Nell and William Neal had made a pretty good cowboy out of Mart. Since Mart came from Irish heritage, he surely indulged in the alcohol diet. If it was swillable, Mart was sure to indulge.

Mart was surely smitten with Mable and courted her at every available chance. This being a prime time for a young woman, she was also dating a fellow from Pearce, Arizona by the name of Pack Lemons. She said she just couldn't make up her mind between the two, however, in the end, Mart Conroy was victorious.

The Ropers Dances were held down near Elfrida, Arizona somewhere between Webb and Double Adobe. In the early 1900s, it was the most popular place for the cowboys and their girls to dance. Back in those days, nearly everyone rode horseback. Families, young and old, would come in buggies or wagons and would usually dance until daylight so they could have day-light to go home by. It seemed as if every dance became a new story for the girls to tell.

Bernice and Pecos's romance had progressed until on Feb 14th, 1912, the year Arizona became a state. They rode to Solomansville, outside of Safford, and were married.

Then, they rode on to the White Mountains for their honeymoon. While they were at White River, Pecos went to work for a butcher shop.

Pecos & Bernice riding to White Mountains

The town was on the Indian reservation, Bernice had a lot of stories she passed on to me. Like, she helped an Indian women birth a baby. When the baby was born, the Indian woman picked it up, walked down to the river and bathed him in the cold water before wrapping him up in his cradleboard. The old lady gave Bernice a pair of beaded rawhide moccasins that we still have today.

Bernice told Pecos they were going to have to think about riding back down to Happy Hollow as she was pregnant with Dale. She wanted to be near her mother who was a midwife and didn't think she wanted to give him his first bath in the White River. They also had to do some more work to prove up on the homestead at Happy Hollow. Pecos had never walked behind his horse and a plow before, but, according to him he succeeded in planting a dry land-field (sic-2) of corn and beans before Dale was born.

He lost little time in getting back to "cowboying." When Dale was about six months old, he landed a good job with a ranch up near Silver City. Both he and Bernice were getting a little tired of dry land farming and were planning to ride up to the Heart Bar ranch in June of 1913. Bernice, at that time, had been riding with Dale on a pillow in front of her. When grandmother Mary heard their plans she pitched a fit. Dale was too little for a horseback trip such as that, and she would keep him until they returned.

The trip to Silver City on horseback was one of many stories that came out when they got to the Gila River. Bernice washed their hot sweaty clothes in the river and we have a picture of her drying the clothes on big flat rocks.

While she was there, she did some remodeling of the bunkhouse at the Heart Bar Ranch by mudding in her window's casements (sic-3) by hand. In the early 1970's she would visit her granddaughter Cgee who was living at the same ranch and took her to show the fingerprints where she had done the remodeling. Pecos said the one thing he remembered about the 130 mile trip to the Heart Bar, was Bernice insisted they put a large plate glass mirror on the pack mule—which we have in the Rockwell house located in Whetstone, Arizona.

She also told about spending a Cowboy Christmas at the neighboring XSX Ranch. A Cowboy Christmas was the biggest, best rootin-tootin (sic-4) party of the year. The XSX Ranch, owned by the Hodges family, was next to the Gila River near the Heart Bar Ranch.

Pecos's pattern was as he would be one of the best cowboys going, but when it came to payday it was time to go to town and "toot it up." Bernice would not join him in this as she wanted to save their money for things she needed at the homestead. It wasn't too long until she was to turn her horse South to go back home to Happy Hollow. Of course Pecos would return, on a promise that he would change his ways for awhile, but soon he would kick over the traces, so to speak, and finally she gave up on him and went to cooking again.

When Dale was in the first grade, Bernice made a harness for his little burro to pull his little red wagon. He would haul water for the Allen school house, *which was Northwest of the Home Place*. It was his first paying job. He and that little burro hauled water all summer long. When payday came along, he was mighty proud that he was earning his keep too.

Dale's 1ˢᵗ paying job

After Mable and Mart were married, Mart filed on a homestead along Turkey Creek. A little spot near a place called Light. It had a post office and Mable became a postmistress. Turkey Creek came from a spring up in the Chirichaua Mountains and ran down into the Sulphur Springs Valley. Years ago, before the Earthquake, it ran all the way to the dry lake outside Wilcox, Arizona.

There was a large hardwood floored dance hall nearby in which Grandmother Mary ran the serving concession. At this time she also raised chickens, sold eggs and butter in Douglas to help make their way. She used to take the old hens that were too old to lay at top speed and would cook them up and make the most delicious pressed chicken sandwiches that you could ever eat. She could not be beat on her chocolate cake and coffee.

Dale, at age eight or nine had his second paying job and he got 25 cents for sweeping out the dance hall and pumping up the dance hall gas lanterns they used for light.

During this time Cheyenne (Chy) Chamberlain came home from the Cavalry. He had a great team of horses and made his living building tanks and working for the ranchers. Grandfather Charles Rathbun had put in a successful dry land farm of corn and maize, and had a chance to prove up on an additional homestead, so he hired Chy to do the work. He rode about 25-30 miles horseback to the Chiricahua Mountains, cut posts and hauled them back by wagon to build fences. Also he built dirt tanks to catch any rain runoff when it came. Then the James Quarters Section became available. Since they had Chy there, Grandpa jumped on this homestead because the James Quarter Section joined his own homestead.

During this time Bernice had gone to a few dances with Chy and they seemed to enjoy each others company. Around this same time, Bernice traded Matty Pressy her Happy Hollow homestead for the Buckwalter's homestead since it also joined Grandpa's land and gave them a big chunk of land totaling around 1,020 acres. The Buckwalters had a two story house and Grandmother was getting rather disillusioned with Grandfather Charles. Since she had Dale to drive her, *(she bought a Model T)* she didn't need Grandpa, so she moved from the old place to the new home place *(Buckwalters)*.

Chy had decided to castrate his big stud horse "Lightning" because he thought he was through with all the horse work that was required for homestead improvements. Grandmother was very frugal, and decided that since Chy was through working, it was time for him to move on. She had been feeding both him and his horses so she sat him down and told him as such. Bernice got mad and told him that this outfit belongs to me and you don't have to move until your horses are well. In the mean time, she had made plans with Nora and Bill Flanders to ride up to the White Mountains on a fishing trip. Chy came in and told Mary his horses were well enough to travel so he would be on his way.

Bernice was getting ready to leave and Grandmother got it into her head that Bernice and Chy were going to run off and get married. She came running out and accused them of this. Dale and Grandfather Charles claimed Mother just said, "that's a pretty good idea, how about it Chy?" Well, shucks, they just all saddled up and went over to Sam Holderman, a Judge, next to the Old Place, and were married. Then Bernice and Chy joined Bill and Nora and they all went to the White Mountains fishing.

Grandmother Mary was throwing such as fit about Bernice and Chy being married that finally Bernice said, "What are you so afraid of? If it doesn't work out its my mistake". Mary was afraid that Chy would make Dale and her move back to the old place, so Bernice said, "If that's all that's bothering you so much, I'll sign the homestead over to you," and she did.

Dale said that Grandmother made Uncle Mart ride all night to Tombstone which was the county seat to record the deed when the court house opened in the morning.

When Bernice and Chy returned from their trip they moved to Douglas where Chy went to work for the smelter moving big houses. They lived in a little house on Green Street just two blocks away from the Mexican border. Bernice's best friend

Lena Schook *(grandmother to Betty Gwen Yeryar)* and her three children lived across the street.

Bernice claimed Chy became disenchanted with his moving job and had heard a lot about jobs in Mexico and wanted to go down and explore some ideas. Bernice said she had always been afraid of Mexico and would not move. Bernice said she believed he had gotten her pregnant with me, *Gale,* thinking she would have to go with him. However, when I was six months old, Chy left for Mexico and my mother Bernice went back to the old place to live with Grandpa Charles.

My earliest memories are all wound around an old Collie dog, "Honeysuckle" climbing up on the old adobe pillars on the front porch and coming out to eat my raw oatmeal and milk in the sunshine. There was also a square cement tank by the windmill for water storage where my Grandfather used to lift me up to get a drink because the water ran cool and clean from the well. From the tank, the water ran into a dirt tank for the cows, chickens, horses and ducks. Grandpa had enough cows so they could sell cream, butter, chickens, and eggs to keep the groceries coming in.

It was not long until Bernice realized she would have to go back to work to make ends meet. Her first job was with the John Riggs family, and she was able to take me with her. The Riggs's had four children of their own, and the only thing I can remember of those early years was, that Jeannette Riggs had a big beautiful porcelain doll behind glass and I was only allowed to look, not touch.

Paul and Stark Riggs talked Ellerbe, the three Riggs boys and me into going out to the big barn to see the new kittens and then they locked Ellerbe and me in the barn. You can imagine how terrified a four year old can get.

It seems to me it became a pattern every time I became ill, Grandmother Mary had to come and get me as my mother was too busy to take care of a sick child.

My memories of our next job were when Mrs. Answorth decided to build the Rancho Manzaneta in Turkey Creek *(now known as El Coronado)*. Mother was hired to cook for the building crew. Once again she started taking me with her, and all went well until Mrs. Answorth, who was quite a drinking lady, got mad at her boyfriend and started shooting at him upstairs where we slept. He jumped over the second story balcony and broke his leg. You can well imagine the impression that makes on a four year old.

Then, I got Whooping Cough and Grandmother had to take me back to the ranch again. Grandmother was also caring for Dale and Tommy Conroy, son of Mable and Mart as well as little old me (Gale).

Grandfather Charles had starved out at the old place and moved over to the home place and lived upstairs. He got a job as the school bus driver and acquired a Model T Touring Car to carry the children. Grandmother Mary took very good care of me but offered very little affection. My Grandfather was always very nice to me. He would hold me on his lap, tell me Bible stories, and always called me his little 'galley'. When my kindergarten age rolled around, my mother was working at the Bar O Dude Ranch outside of Tombstone. She again took me with her. The Kendall's, who owned the ranch, had three daughters. The youngest, Mollie, was my age and they made a deal with one of their guests who was a New York school teacher named Madeline to home school their children. I was included and really loved all the things she taught Mollie and me to do.

As the pattern continued, I got the flu and Grandmother had to come for me once more.

Dale graduated from the 8th grade in Ash Creek when I started the first grade. Since we had lost Uncle Mark in 1927, Tommy had gone to be with his mother Mable, who was working for Lillian Riggs at the Faraway Ranch and started a boy's school for wealthy boys.

Somewhere during this time is when Pecos came back to Sulfur Springs Valley to try to talk Bernice into going back to the White Mountains and to try it again. I was eight years old. Two things I remember so plain; there was something going on between them that I didn't understand.

We had all gone to Ike Price's for a summer rodeo. Dale was roping and we were all watching him. He rode up and told his dad, Pecos, that I am a little short of cash to enter the next go-round, do you have any money? Pecos put his hand in his pocket and pulled a handful of change. Dale said, "Hell if I didn't have any more than that I would throw it away." Pecos pitched it into the nearest Mesquite bush.

That night was the first time I remember seeing my mother Bernice dance. At that time I had a terrible crush on a good looking cowboy but he was too old to see me. Many years later I was able to tell him how good looking I thought he was back then.

One evening soon after the rodeo, Bernice and Dale were busy packing up his Model A. The next morning about 4:00am we left. I remember when we went through Willcox to gas up, the station had the radio playing and it was telling about the Lindbergh baby being kidnapped. That night, late, we pulled into the Morris Ranch where we were to live for almost a year.

Pecos met us. He got off, propped me on his horse, got in with Bernice and Dale and told me to follow them. That was my first ride by myself on a strange horse. I was scared but I wouldn't let anyone know that.

Pecos took care of the ranch for the Morris' who were getting old in exchange for our little house on the hill. Then he worked on the road during the week for the Workman's Public Assistance (WPA).

We had arrived sometime in early June because I had my 9th birthday there. Bernice had invited the neighborhood children; Mittie, Emily and Clyde Brown to my party. She did that so I would know some of the children when I started school in

Pinyon about four miles from the ranch. That summer Pecos turned me loose on a little stubborn Shetland pony bareback and believe me she taught me how to ride. When it came time to ride to school, Pecos arranged for Clyde Brown to stay with us so we could ride to school together. We were riding double on a little grey mare that was balky and always wanted to go back to the barn. Pecos would get behind her with his "catchrope" (sic-5) and whip her until we went

over the hill out of sight of the barn. Clyde and I would be leaning really far forward for fear Pecos might miss with his catchrope.

The next summer it was moving day again. Bernice and Pecos had traded for a little place about five miles away. It was an old homestead consisting of 160 acres without any house, just a well dug in the middle of a flat (sic-6). Bernice managed to make a foundation of rocks from the surrounding country-side. She put only enough flooring to hold our cook stove and our beds. Our beds had old fashioned metal bedsteads that she would drape a tarp over. She also traded a right-away (sic) for the logging-train to cross the ranch for a couple of dilapidated houses in MacNary. Dale and Ralph Parker tore down those houses, loaded them on the logging-train and hauled them out to the where the right-away crossed the homestead. My job that summer, was to straighten **all** the nails from the lumber so Bernice would then have them ready the following day. She just built the house around the cook stove and beds. I don't believe there was a day that summer that we didn't have rain showers and a little hail with it. I was away from camp helping Pecos' brother Fred build a pasture fence. One time we didn't get back before it was pouring rain. Bernice had the house up and the fireplace built by the time school started.

It wasn't long before Fred decided that his mother needed him back in Pecos, Texas. He claimed it was too tough a life for him.

Pecos had traded for a little sorrel mare for me named Dollie and she was a git-up-and-go little dude and I loved her. I rode her bareback to school so when the snow came I was a lot warmer. The following summer I found a new friend, her name was Maureen Butler, and we found we could ride part way to school together and that made the trip a lot more fun.

Those years at the Buckhorn Ranch, as we called it after Pecos' brand, seemed to go by in a hurry. We were to build the barn, a round bronc corral with a holding chute, and somehow during all the construction, Pecos got in about 40 acres of corn crop.

He had gotten a job gathering wild horses for the U.S. Government off the Indian Allotment for wild horses. I thought there was nothing to match the joy of running wild horses through forest trees, and bushes. This was especially true where the McNary Saw Mill was located, and the loggers had finished logging. Pecos and I had to have horses that could jump a downed log going at a full run.

Pecos brought home a boy by the name of Tom Casey to help break out the wild horses. He gave Tom and me four horses apiece to break and teach to rein. When we were done training them, we would show and sell them, then start on four more.

Bernice had built a bunkhouse out of railroad ties, and then made Pecos haul her in some soil which she used to plaster the inside as you would with plaster today.

You can well imagine money to work with was pretty scarce since it was depression time. However, Bernice did manage enough for some chickens, and we also had a good milk cow. Then there were also squirrels and occasionally we'd go fishing.

One summer, the Babbitt brothers started sending several bands of sheep through our place to the high country, and they continued this practice every summer after. One time, the herder lost a whole band of five hundred sheep. I had been out hunting horses when I ran into them and I came home to tell Pecos about them. Well, we went back, brought them back & put them in a pen, then rode into Pinetop and called the Babbitts. They assured us they would send someone for them if we could keep them for a couple of days. I had to get up early to feed and bring them in at night. When they came for the flock, they gave me twenty-five sheep for taking care of them.

We were meat hungry and I sure did love the taste of that mutton. Pecos had been a butcher early in life and had to know how to butcher sheep or your meat would taste funny.

Sometime each summer, Emily Michener, who had a Guest Ranch with about 25 girls, would hire Pecos to lead them on pack trip about 30 miles from the ranch to Mt. Orad. One summer, Pecos took me along. We would all sit around the campfire and tell stories and poems. Pecos was a poet and taught me several even though I was only 10 and the girls loved them. I still remember them and have been called upon to recite them today.

Pecos also saved a little paint stud that would buck and bawl that he kept for me to ride with a "circingle" (sic-7) for show to entertain the girls. We took him to a rodeo and they passed the hat and I got enough money for my first permanent. I was always after Pecos to let me break him gentle as he was such a pretty paint horse, and I named him Rags. Pecos said maybe, if I would ride with a saddle, which I didn't like, I might be able to keep him from bucking. I set about breaking him riding a saddle and thought I was doing pretty well until one day Pecos and I went up Brown Creek looking for wild horses. We had to pass some friends, the Penrods, and Mrs. Penrod came out to talk with us. She told Pecos he was going to get me killed riding that little horse as she has seen him buck at the rodeo. Pecos told her she had him in her pile (cowboy language for ramuda [sic-8]).

We jumped a bunch of wild horses and ran those Cayuses (sic) about five miles before they kind of settled down. Pecos got down and pulled his saddle off his horse to let him cool off and blow (sic). He always told me you don't ask why, you just watch and learn, so I did what he did. After about 30 minutes he saddled up getting ready to ride again so I did too. However, when I started to get on Rags he jumped out from under me and I landed behind the saddle, and the next jump I hit the dust. Pecos was cussing saying, "What are you trying to do, run our horses away again?" He got down, caught Rags and said, "get on him kid." He was holding his head and earing (sic-9) him down. This time Rags really turned on, threw Pecos' hold on his ear loose, threw me off again, and kicking me on my forehead blackening both eyes. I know Pecos was scared of what was happening to me, but you wouldn't have known it as he was cussing so loud.

His horse had broken loose and ran off with Rags and joined the wild horses and left us about 10 miles from home and afoot. Fortunately his horse's rains got tangled up in some brush, we found him after we had trailed them for about an hour. We caught up to the wild horses and he roped Rags. This time he snubbed (sic-10) him up to his saddle horn and I got back on. That how the little horse found he could be rode and quit bucking with me. Needless to say this was one day we rode home without the wild horses as they got away.

In the 15 years I owned Rags, I was never able to ride him bare back because he would buck and bawl like he did before I broke him to the saddle. If I tried to ride him bareback, he would buck, and bawl like I was killing the poor animal. The only way I could get him home was to get off and lead him home. Sometimes it was long walk.

I think it was the summer I was 12, that Grandmother Mary Rathbun and Dale came up to visit us. When she saw Bernice, she told her she had to go home to the old ranch, East of Pearce, with them to see the doctor. She recognized the signs that

Bernice was very ill. We thought she was just tired and cranky. Bernice returned with them to see the doctor.

The doctor said she had an inward goiter that would have killed her in six months and she needed surgery.

I had stayed home with Pecos because it was wild horse season again. Though I was too young to realize it, Pecos had begun drinking again while Bernice was gone. We would come in after a hard day and he would say lets ride to Pinetop and see if we had heard anything from your mother Bernice. Then he would leave me with some friends, Clara Rhodes and the Renfro's while he went drinking. We would ride home about 1:00am in the morning. Pecos would say he was waiting for the moon to come up so we could see our way home.

The most I can recall about this time was the groceries were pretty scarce. He would put on a pot of beans and make a batch of biscuits while I did the milking and that was about all I had to live on. One time he had a jug of wine and he went off to Pinetop by himself and left me alone til the next morning.

The next morning Tom Casey drove out in a yellow convertible with a rumble seat. He loaded us up and we headed for Sulfur Springs Valley to get Bernice. The roads were not paved then and I remember it had gotten very dark and the car ahead of us had slipped off the road. Pecos and Tom stopped and were helping them get back on the road. Of course Pecos was talking and cussing and I heard the man ask you wouldn't be Pecos Higgins would you sir. "You damned right," said Pecos, "how did you know." The man said, "I just heard someone say that Pecos Higgins could talk and cuss louder than anyone in the state of Arizona so I figgured you must be him."

After that incident on the trip, we were driving out of Safford to the Valley and it had rained so the road was slick. Tom told Pecos to jump out and push. I was in the rumble seat and they thought I was asleep as it was about 4:00 in the morning but I jumped out and was pushing too when the car got a little traction and took off without me. I guess they didn't hear me yell. Later Tom said do you hear Gale? When they stopped to check if I was ok, they figured I must be back in the muddy area.. Here I was way back down the road hollering, "Don't leave me!" They backed up and picked up a mud splattered, wet little gal. I was tempted to use some of Pecos' cuss words but I was afraid he might hear me so I just kept hollering.

What I had not known at the time, was that Pecos sold all our cows to buy a car he couldn't drive, to come to the Valley to pick up Bernice. I'm sure when she came back with us she was very unhappy because she had tried so hard to make a home for us and get ahead. I am pretty sure he must have promised her he would quit drinking again too . . .

13 Year Old Gale's 312 Mile Ride

Iᴛ ᴡᴀs ᴛʜᴀᴛ ꜰᴀʟʟ that Bernice suggested that I should go down to Grandmother Mary's for school so I wouldn't have to ride through heavy snow. She must have worried that her and Pecos wouldn't make it. We all sat down that evening, drew a map for me. The next morning I left with one dress, a five dollar bill for a Valley some 312 miles away. Pecos wouldn't let me ride my little paint horse because he would give out about the second or third day and in turn gave me his old favorite, Calico who was 17 years old at the time, and he knew he would make the trip.

Pecos told others that the light of his life went out as he watched the old paint horse and his little girl leave. I was 13 years old and mother and I figured if I remained at home in Pineyon, Arizona, I would have to ride a total of 1,380 miles to and from school in the extreme cold of the northern pine country. On the other hand, if I went to Grandmother Mary's down in Pearce, I would only have to ride 312 miles in one hop so I decided to take it all at once.

I left at 5:00 am on August 29th and my excess baggage was one dress, one sweater and $5.00 in expense money. The first part of the journey was through the vast pine forests and rugged mountains of the Chiricaua. Apache Reservation   The first night, I spent in Fort Apache at White River with the Stockman (sic-11) and his wife.

The trip had been planned that I would spend the second night with John Moore at the Black River Ranch. However, the White River folks got me up early so I arrived shortly after noon. When I got to the Black River Ranch, no one was around. It appeared no one had been there for some time. While looking around the Ranch, I saw a highway sign that indicated the Hilltop Sawmill was only eighteen miles up the road. That's where we had planned to spend night number three. I decided to go for it. It made a pretty rough trip for Calico, but he was fresh and made it by dark like a champion.

Pecos had given me a note to his friend at the Hilltop Sawmill, but I discovered they had moved away three years before. So I hunted up the local Stockman, Hibrown and his wife. They took me in and gave me a good bed and took care of Calico. The Next morning, after breakfast, they sent me on my way with a great lunch.

On the way to San Carlos, I met an old Indian who told me, because I was not wearing a hat, he thought I should wear his beaded head band so I wouldn't get heat stroke. I still have his gift today. I continued through the mountainous reservation and arrived at San Carlos, Arizona.

I had a letter from Pecos to his old friend, Black Jack Trainer, to introduce me as his daughter. In the mean time, Black Jack had married a High Society gal who didn't take it kindly when I showed up on that Indian pony with a beaded head band and told her, "I was supposed to spend the night." Her reply was, "I don't think so!" She went back into the house, and came back with Black Jack who told me to follow him. He took me down to the San Carlos Stockman and his wife and asked them to put me up for the night.

They were wonderful to me. His wife even took my travel clothing and washed them so could start off nice and clean in the morning.

Black Jack came up in the morning and told me I should take a shorter route to Bylas, by crossing Coolidge Dam up higher. He thought it would cut off 30 mile going the way we had planned.

However, mother and Pecos wanted me to follow the main highway so I missed the turn Black Jack told me about.

Black Jack must have been worried about me, because he caught up with me 18 miles past the turn. He took his brand new Stetson off and gave it to me because I was getting in to the hot, dry desert country. Then he told me I should try to stay at Coolidge Dam that night. When I rode up to the dam, I didn't find any place for Calico or any hay for him, so I bought a candy bar and one Delaware Punch. Then, I continued on my way. It soon got too hot to hold the bottle so I finished it and threw it away.

One of Pecos' old friend from Bylas had gone to San Carlos with a load of pigs to sell at auction. Black Jack told him I was on my way and if he could pick me up in his pick up it would be a great help. By the time they over took me on the road, Calico was getting pretty hot and tired. They explained what Black jack had told them and I told them that Calico had never been loaded into a vehicle before. But Calico was for anything but having to head back down that road, even the smell of pigs wouldn't deter him.

They didn't have any side-boards on the back of the truck, so after we got him up and in to the back of the truck, I rode back there holding on to him. All went well until we drove under a railroad bridge, and he became frightened. Calico tried to climb out and in so doing slashed my shoulder with his front hoofs. They stopped the truck and helped me get him down and I rode the last ten miles to the Bert Hinton Ranch in Bylas. I spent that night at the Ranch.

Safford was only about twenty miles, so we were going to have an easy day. However, Pecos did not have anyone to refer me to. He thought that by then, I would sort of know my way around. I rode up to the biggest barn of hay beside the road, and asked if Calico and I could spend the night? At first, they were hesitant because they thought I was a runaway. But, when I explained my trip and destination, they were the nicest people you could meet. I had asked them to get me up really early the next morning because Wilcox was sixty miles away. They felt sorry for me and let me sleep in. Gave me a big lunch and sent me on my way. There are lots of people named John in Safford, but I'll sure have to tip my hat to this family for being among the best.

About noon I spotted a windmill beside the highway and decided to stop and rest and water Calico.. While I was there, a big truck loaded with hay spotted me and stopped. One guy was an old cowboy, Slim Harper, who told his driver to break a bail of hay and feed it to Calico. He didn't have anything with him for me except a bottle of bourbon that I had to decline. Later, I was very well acquainted with the Harpers and their family.

When it started to cool off, I climbed up and we started again. By dark, we had reached a spot in the highway that was parallel with the SP Railroad.   The lights of the train would blind us so I let Calico wear the Stetson. We didn't get into Wilcox until around 2:00 am so I stayed at the first Auto Court I found. I staked out Calico in the tall green grass and during the night I got up several times to re-stake him. Would you believe those blood sucker charged me $1.00 for half a night on a hard bed and no food.

The next day was to be the final one on my trip so we took it easy. I stopped at Cochise, bought some hay for Calico, a candy bar for me and we started on. I was almost to Pearce when a big truck stopped. It seems they had passed me up near Stafford. When they saw me again, they stopped and talked to me. It turned out they were my Grandmother Mary's nearest neighbors. Needless to say, by this time, Calico was ready to ride any thing on wheels. We loaded him on the truck and took off. It was just about twelve miles to the ranch. They pulled the truck into a ditch a hundred yards from the gate and unloaded

Calico. I remounted, and with a fine sense of drama, I finished my trip by racing to Grandmothers whooping at the top of my lungs.

My Grandfather had heard the noise while we were unloading and wondered what was happening. When he saw me, and the little Indian pony, with my hair splaying out behind like a blanket in the wind, he asked my Grandmother, "Is it an Indian, is it an Indian?" Grandmother knew who I was, but she did not know that I had ridden down. She thought the truck had brought me down from the White Mountains. When she found out what really happened, she really *Blessed* out my mother, and said, "Bernice never really had any sense." Calico and I were really happy to be back home. Along the way I talked to several tourists and obligingly posed for snapshots several times

. One of those folks was a Mrs. Carter, who was a friend of Reg Manning of the Republican Gazette in Phoenix. He wrote to me asking me for the story of my trip.

My Aunt Mable was working at a Guest Ranch called the El Coronado where a Mrs. Dean was staying. She was the wife of the President of general Motors Corp. and also a renowned author on her own. When she hear of the story, she requested an interview.

It was decided she would just send the interview to Reg Manning at the newspaper. When she found out he was a cartoonist, she was afraid no one would believe my story.

See letters after cartoons of trip

Later, when I was in High School, an old man came out to board with my mother at the mine. When he saw the framed picture of my ride on the wall, he asked her who that was. She told him that the story was about her daughter Gale's ride. He told her that he was sitting on a park bench in Miami, Florida, when he read the story in the local newspaper, and told mother he always wanted to meet a real western gal. That story must have been sent all over the country—WOW!

The trip took me six days, and along the road, I got fruit from friendly people and I also had a fine 10 gallon hat. I arrived at Grandmother's with $2.75 of the original $5.00 making a total expense for the entire 312 miles of $2.25. How about that, Pilgrim?

The following cartoon drawing of my trip was drawn up by Reg Manning and he put it in the paper along with my story. It was just too big for the book so I added it in the next three pages. . .

GALE'S RIDE

PART 1

Part 2

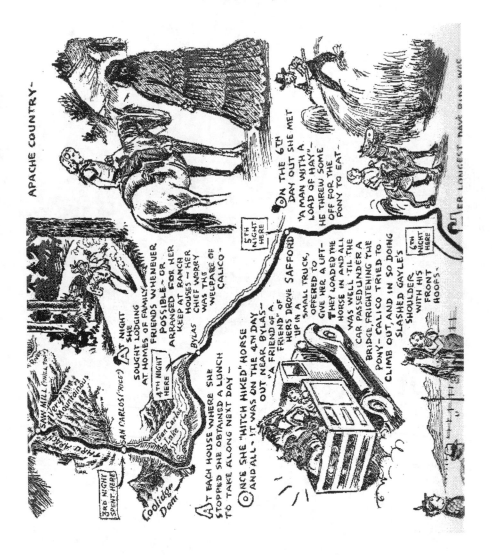

42

PART 3

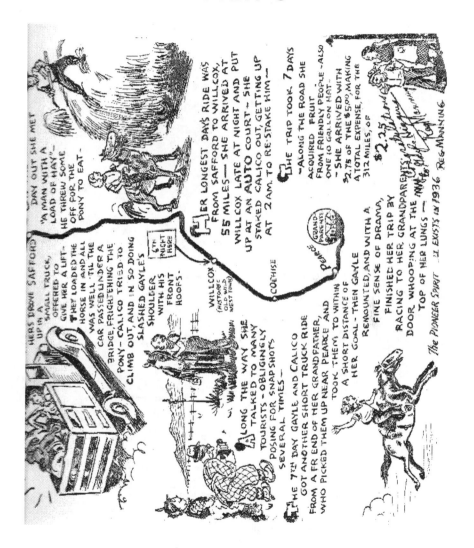

Yes, you'll have to splice the images to see the whole dang thing. But I figure y'all can do that just fine.

PHOENIX REPUBLIC AND GAZETTE

September 19, 1936.

Miss Gale Higgins
c/o C. C. Rathburn
Rathburn Ranch
Pearce, Arizona

Dear Miss Higgins:

I have a letter from Mr. Reagan Carter of Winslow in
which he tells me you recently made a 250 mile trip alone
by horseback from McNary to Pearce. I wonder if you would
like to write me a letter describing your trip. Perhaps
it would be easier for you if I were to ask you questions,
then you can just answer them.

1. Did you make this trip alone all the way?
2. How many days did it take you to make the trip?
3. Where did you sleep? When? (Please tell about each place
   you slept)
4. Did you prepare any of your own meals?
5. Did you travel along the highway all the way? (I am enclosing a highway map, will you mark the route you
   traveled and return it to me?)
6. Were you ever frightened? If so tell about it.
7. Do you have a picture of yourself and your pony? If
   not, a picture of you alone will do. If you prefer you
   can have someone take a roll of snapshots and send them
   to me. I can develop them here.
8. What experiences thrilled you most about your trip?
9. Please tell anything else about your trip that you like.
   Don't be afraid to write a long letter. I will be glad
   to hear anything you have to tell.

Mr. Carter was very enthused over the story of your trip
as he heard it. Of course, I do not know just what use I
shall make of any material that you send. If you verify his
story it is probable that I will "draw it up" in the Big
Parade, but of course I can't be sure until I have read
your reply. I will write you again after I have read your
reply.

I would sincerely appreciate hearing from you.

Sincerely yours,

Reg Manning:om
encl

REG MANNING

44

Nov. 28, 1936

Miss Gayle Higgins
  Pearce, Ariz.

Dear Miss Higgins:
              Enclosed are the films
you sent me together with prints of them
I thought you'd like to have.
              I suppose you have
received the drawing and Big Parade pages
I sent you. I thought you might like
that original drawing for your collection.
              I certainly appreciate
the fine letter you sent describing your
adventures and hope you were pleased
with the outcome. That was a good poem
too, but as you could see, I just didn't
have the space to use it.
                  Thanks again —
                    REG MANNING

Shortly after my trip, Bernice found a job cooking for a logging crew at the MacNary sawmill. She had to save money to pay for her surgery. The next summer I went to spend my vacation with her at the logging camp. It was surely a fun summer as Pecos came over, brought over my little paint horse and another for a companion. We were at Hannegans Meadow, and there was a lot of green food there for them. I could hobble the horses and have an extra horse for my friends to ride.

Summer ended and it was back to school in the Valley. Later on, I figured Bernice made a trip to the Buckhorn and discovered that Pecos had sold the windows out of the house for another quart of whiskey. This time she called Dale who loaded up her bed, my horse and came back to the Valley for good.

Life Beyond High School

THEN IT WAS ON to High School at Pearce. These days were filled with work on the ranch and working for neighbors for a little spending money for dances, rodeos, and fun. The year I graduated from Pearce, I went to Douglas to live with my Aunt Mable and take a post-graduate course. I wanted to become a Photo-Journalist but the summer before I enrolled, I had my "bucking horse" fall flat with me aboard and I suffered a bad concussion. This led to my fainting spells in school. The School invited me to go home and recover before returning to school.

My brother was working his mines over in Nogales and his partner, Lee West, who was a retired Chiropractor, felt sure part of my problem, was a cracked vertebrae. Lee was able to adjust my back and keep me in trim until my fainting spells disappeared.

Thelma, was Lee's daughter who was at the mining camp with us. We two shared the cook tent, Lee and Dale had the other tent.. One day our little Butane stove flamed up and the flame was reaching up to the top of the tent. Thelma ran out side. Since we had to haul our water, I walked over to the Butane tank and unhooked it, and pitched it clear over to the dump where it exploded and knocked Thelma on her butt.

Dale was irritated because he had to go to town to get another tank. Lee smiled and said, "Blondie (me) just knew what to do because it could have burned up both our gear and tents."

During this time, WWII was getting pretty intense, and since we hadn't struck it rich, we all move back to Douglas. All of us went to work at the Airport where I met my husband where he was in flight training to become a fighter pilot.

I thought I was through writing this darn book along time ago until everyone started saying they wanted to hear more of my story. So, with the acquisition of a new husband, Pete Ginn, I figured I should elaborate about our life in the little town of Bonita, Louisiana.

When Pete first came back from overseas, we were sent to Miami Beach, Florida for a month before he was re-assigned to Galveston, Texas.

This was truly an experience I hadn't had as yet. We were all located in Government Trailer Housing when a Hurricane blew in. The boys were all ordered to fly their airplanes to safer air fields. The wives and children were left to fend for ourselves. We went to a school cafeteria located in the basement to ride out the Hurricane. When it was over, our trailer park had not been hit. Some of the girls were not so lucky; their trailers had either been flattened or blown a way.

After Galveston, TX it was on to Alexandria, LA. This was a little town with five military bases in the immediate area. There wasn't any place we could rent a room much less a house.

I have failed to mention, that when Pete was flying, he was playing Bridge for ½ cent a point. Pete had photographic memory when it came to cards so we lived off his winnings and banked his paycheck. After a bit, we found a little two bedroom house in Alexandria and rented out our second bedroom.

During this time, we had a terrific flood. The Red River overflowed its banks and this old gal had never seen so much water. I went down town and bought some rope, a hatchet, and four inner tubes. I really got laughed at, but in this case they sent the boys out with the planes, and I made up my mind to make a raft for CGee and me because I AM A SURVIVOR!

Pete had survived being shot down three times flying B-17s over Germany's Europe and finished his 50 mission requirement. This earned him the Silver Star, Distinguished Flying Cross, the Soldier's Medal along with the Silver Boot for getting out of North Africa.

The Pacific War was heating up pretty good so they began training Pete as a B-29 Pilot. Pete could see the Army sending him to serve in the Pacific Theater and since he was the High point man on base because of his European tour, he decided to get out of the Army Air Corps.

After Alexandria we moved to Bonita and we bought Pete's mother and father an old Southern Plantation home and Pecan Orchard. We were lucky enough to get into the Café and bar business and soon we were back on our feet. It was hard to keep Pete home because his gambling blood began to boil and I was stuck running both the bar and café.

We had a Calvary Distillery Mill in our town, and all the young workers would come to eat and party with us. I didn't seem to fit with a lot of the folks Pete travel with (The Upper Crust). I organized a baseball team to play every Sunday. The boys would either go fishing or hunting so I could throw a big fry after our games. I was told that after I left Louisiana, my team won the State Championship. I was proud of my boys!

It was while I was there that Dale had written that his dad, Pecos, was in prison over a calf incident and that Pecos had put me on his mailing list. I wrote to Pecos to see if there was anything I could do to help him. His reply was, "They only furnish us with Bull Durham (sic-12) smokes here and you know that I like Prince Albert or Velvet (sic-13). If you could send me enough money each month for candy bars I'd be set.

I'm here in Florence and it's nice and warm and I won't have to fight that White Mountain snow. They put me out on a horse ranch and I have one of the prettiest colts you've ever seen. They don't know it but they are doing me one hell of a favor! It was during this time that I wrote Pecos and asked him to write the story of Calico. I also suggested that he write his life story if he had the time. Pecos did this for me, and at the end of the story he thanked the Prison Warden for allowing him to send the stories to me.

One day a boy came into the bar and wanted a five gallon Tom Collins. Now Pete had cut off this old boy's credit so I was in a quandary till he held up a new 22 Springfield rifle and offered it in payment for the bill. I wrote "Paid In Full" across the top. This was one of the highlights of Louisiana for me cause I used to go out into the Bayous and shoot Water Moccasins sunning themselves on the swamp logs.

On one of Pete's gambling trips, he must have been lucky cause he came home with 50 head of long yearling bulls. He was drunk as a skunk, and told everyone that his wife was a cow gal and he'd bought her some cows. We had eight acres of Pecan trees to put them to pasture. The out come, was one great (sic-14) "Rocky Mountain Oyster" supper. After they were branded they were turned out into the Bayous to fend for themselves.

Pete and I had a pretty good working relationship. He did not mind that I worked with the mill boys building my baseball team for most of the boys had girl friends that would help out with our fries. I had a huge cast iron wash pot that we put on a bon fire to heat the oil for French fries, etc.

One evening, Pete came in to help me close the bar and café and seemed to want to visit. This was unusual for him. He said, "Gale, on one of my parties in New Orleans, I guess I got to drunk and it seems I got a little girl in trouble. She wants us to adopt the baby. I told her I would talk it over with you. You know we wanted another one to go with our daughter CGee.

I'm sure that CGee was the greatest love of his life. I told him That I would think about it, but I did not think so. But I wouldn't leave him because of this which seemed to be his greatest fears.

Louisiana was a strange country to me. It seems the wives just seemed to expect this kind of behavior from their husbands. It appeared acceptable for their husbands to fool around with what they termed (sic-15) High Yellows. That was one habit that I balked at, and I told him that if that ever happened, that would be all she ever wrote for us.

CGee had her forth birthday when I happened to go to the café at 2:30 am because I had forgotten her ear ache medication. When I got there, I found Pete and my colored dishwasher in the bedroom upstairs and they weren't washing dishes.

The next morning I didn't fuss, I just packed up CGee and our stuff and left the State of Louisiana for good.

Pete thought that I'd be back once I cooled off. Pete didn't just didn't realize there are some things I would not put up with and he crossed the line. There was no way I'd go back with him . . .

When I hit Douglas at first, I stayed with my Aunt Mable again. Then My dad, Chy, who had moved back out of Mexico and bought a little house in Douglas. He offered it to me and CGee. He said he was with the Border Patrol and had been reassigned to Canao down by Nogales. I said that I appreciated his offer.

I went to work for George Hennigan at a dairy for about a year. CGee and I settled in at 1415 15th Street in Douglas. That's when riding as a double in the movies started.

A local vet was very aware of my riding abilities. He told the Director to pick the girl that was wearing the Mexican coat my mother had made it for me, and it was quite colorful. There were several girls trying out for the part, but I was chosen and had to join the wranglers union as did the others who did riding and were extras.

New experiences seem to be my way of life. The money was good and Paramount offered me a permanent job, but I thought Hollywood was a rough life for a country cal and I had a four year daughter to raise. I worked a couple more movies when they came out to our location, but I have never been sorry that I did not go to Hollywood.

Gale working in the movies

Old Movie Poster

Gale was the stunt rider for Shelly Winters

GALE'S MOVIE STORIES

Y'ALL HAVE BEEN AFTER me to talk about myself and to be honest, there isn't that much I think you'd be interested in, but you asked so, here goes:

As you can see from the posters above, I really did do some riding in few movies:

I worked on several western movies as riding double. One I remember because it was a lot of fun was called Branded. Alan Ladd and Mona Freeman were the stars.

Gale is 2nd from right top row

The wranglers on the picture "Branded"

Branded was the first movie that I did riding doubles in. I already told you I was chosen, but I thought you'd like to hear about a few of the funny things that go on behind the scenes.

They have these little tin crosses that they nail to the ground so when you bring your horse in at a dead run you'll know exactly where to stop. Sometimes we had to re-shoot a scene to get what they wanted. Ever try to stop a running horse in just the right place? One of my friends was a sitting up on a fence post and they reshot the same scene for three days with him sitting on that post til they were happy.

Then, here was one scene up on a hill in a different location. There were a lot of (sic-16) catclaw bushes scattered all over that hillside. Alan Ladd and I were to come down that hill at a dead run. I was wearing a riding skirt and the catclaws caught my skirt and pulled it above my knees.

The next day the Director made the whole darn crew go back and re-shot that scene. He told me I had to keep my skirt down so I had to kind of pick my way down at a run and keep away from those bushes. On 0ne of those re-shoots, Alan Ladd told me he wished he could ride with the ease that I did. I told him that if he had ever put as many miles on horse back that I had he probably could. He was one star that liked to do his own riding if possible.

On one take when we were riding up to the Cochise Stronghold, the wind was blowing so hard it caught my hat and blew it across my face. Yep, you guessed it; we had to re-shoot the run again and again. That was how our Director worked for perfection.

When I told him I didn't like Western Movies because they ran the horses all the time. He explained that he had to tell a complete story in a little time so we couldn't be moseying down the trail. I could understand his point of view but I didn't have to like it as it was hard on the horses.

One thing I got a kick out of was my horse had a stand in. Sheba was a mare I rode for the running scenes and Sheik did all the stills — he was a stallion. I'll bet a lot of western kids knew the difference when they watched these movies.

Mona Freeman was a darling girl to work with but she was scared to death of horses. Mona refused to get on one even for stills.

I remember in one scene, Alan was leaving and I was to try to catch him as I ran my horse down the hill and I was to holler "WAIT!" Would you believe they paid me $50.00 for that one word?

This was truly an experience for a country gal.

When I went to work for Universal Pictures with Joseph Cotton and Shelly Winters as a riding double, it was in February and cold. The first day we went out on location, it was an unusually warm day. Shelly Winters made the director write into the script where she took her coat off and hung it on the corral gate. The next day it snowed and in the picture she was wearing a frilly thin white blouse. After the snow, the makeup artist had to take special care with my makeup as Shelly would not come out of her trailer. In one scene, her father was supposed to have been shot, so I had to ride up, jump down and pick up his head as he died. It took two days of shooting the scene because he couldn't lie still long enough to die. This movie was 'Untamed Frontier'.

One incident I remember so well; our costume lady was a little heavy but a wonderful person. She was dressed for cold weather. She was wearing pants, sweater and a heavy jacket when she went out to the port-a-potty. While doing her business, a whirlwind came up and turned it over.

We all heard a shout, "Help me, PLEASE help me." Gurtha was not hurt, just her pride for being caught with her pants down and her girdle showing. She was such a great sport, we all laughed the incident off.

I found that Movie People really love to party especially when they are on location. Most of them were staying at the Gadston Hotel in Douglas, AZ. It had an excellent restaurant and a large cowboy bar with western music and a great dance floor. They really did make this place come alive while they were there. For example, one morning there was a rumor among the movie folks, that Joseph Cotton was having so much fun that before he made it to bed, he slipped and injured his back. He had to be taken by stretcher to the train to go back to California for treatment.

Our Douglas Dispatch carried a story that he had been injured rescuing a little girl in a run-away wagon. I seemed the Douglas location was shorted because the crew ended up shooting just a few scenes that Joe was not in.

They offered to take me with them as a regular member of the crew. But being just a country girl with a four year old little girl of my own, I thought it would be rough life. You must know that that kind of money back in those days had to be really tempting.

Moving right along, let me take you back to my little house in Douglas.

My mother had retired in Cochise so I let CGee go live with her and I continued to work and helped her whenever I could. My mother Bernice and Thelma worked so I could get job driving the Cochise School Bus. I closed my little house in Douglas and moved to in with my mother.

One Saturday, my present boyfriend came to take me to a dance in Wilcox. That night I spied a tall red headed cowboy who had the prettiest shirt I had ever seen. H also looked like the best dancer on the floor. My boyfriend said, "Is you neck on a swivel tonight?" I told him that was the prettiest shirt I'd ever seen. He also accused me of flirting with others, so that night he said, "I know that guy and he wouldn't give you the second look. And he even offered to introduce me to him." I said, "If you do, I'll own that shirt in six months."

I had some mutual friends that owned a local bar. One night, Buck was a little more sober. He asked my friends about me and they told him I wouldn't give him the time of day. We both must have loved a challenge and ended up with each other.

My mother and daughter CGee dearly loved Buck drunk or sober and always made excuses when he messed up. I have mentioned Buck in many of my short stories and kind of introduce him to you. He nearly starved me to death because he just couldn't handle money. But he surely made life interesting.

Buck and our adventures took us to live on Catalina Island off the coast of California for over a year. Buck was recruited 900 head of old mossy horned Brahma bulls who were supposed to have been castrated when they were yearlings. The managed to escape the island barge and end up covered the island as there was ample feed and springs all over the place.

The island is so steep that even some of the cattle had fallen to their death. Buck soon saw they could not be (sic-17) cowboyed off. He started off in the jeep with a load of sweet feed. He would spread some out and then beat on the side of the jeep to get their attention. They soon became accustomed to the sound and the feed left behind. After a few months, he was able to entice them down to the shipping pens to eat. At long last were boarded on the barges back to the mainland.

After removing the bulls, Buck's job turned into hunting. The island was covered with wild goats, mule footed pigs an 80 Buffalo brought over for some filming. Buck would dress out about ten goats every day to go to Avalon where the Wrigley's had the largest birds Avery in the world. A lot of these birds were meat eaters. The island goat population furnished their meals.

While we were there, we were all recruited to help Howard Hill (a world famous Archer) making a movie advertising the line of Ben Person bow and arrows. When he left, he gave Buck an eighty pound bow with 24 arrows which Buck made our lives pretty exciting as he zeroed in around us.

After the island our adventures took us to the top of California on ranches and then back to the deserts of El Centro. Buck worked in a feed yard there for several months before we returned to Arizona.

When we returned to the old ranch he found a new vocation of well drilling. That took care of us for the next 3-4 years. We drilled irrigation well on the ranch that was so successful the Texas farmers began buying up the land around us for farming. This was more than Buck could take so he left his son and CGee with me and went back to New Mexico to his cowboy way of life.

After Buck flew the coop I had to find a way to make a living in order for CGee to finish High School. I worked part time as the Post Mistress in Pearce then the old German lady who ran the general store needed help and I volunteered. I also put in 40 acres of maize and 10 acres of baby lima beans. Since I did not have the equipment, I had to trade bookkeeping for a farmer to get my crop plowed and planted. Then it was up to me to keep it watered and weeded.

Meantime I took a bartending job in Wilcox at night. Before the year was over my water pump gave out and I was forced to ride an old Soward race horse in a matched race to get the money to fix it. This turned out a little different than I had planned. I was riding one of Bing Crosby's old race horses who jumped the race track and hit a car that was lined up for a fence. I came out of this wreck with a broken knee, elbow and crushed pelvis. My neighbor told me not to worry about my crop and took care of it for me. And when I paid back all the money I had put in to it, I had made eight dollars profit.

After this I was back to bartending and bookkeeping. I moved to Tucson and worked as a cashier in a truck stop for three years. Then I was called home to care for my mother who had had surgery at 80 and the doctor told me to take her home. Make her comfortable and happy as she probably didn't have 30 days left. She lived ten more years and one more surgery so I must have been a good care giver.

From then on, it seemed to me my job was to take care of all our old and sick relatives. When I thought I had run the gauntlet I was called to Las Cruces because my daughter was ill. I had to sell the ranch in order to take care of my mother and I had one payment left on it. I bought a small acreage in Dona Ana and put my mobile home on it to begin a new adventure.

I boarded horses and worked for an antique dealer. I also worked as a care taker for several years until I arrived at the age of 62, when Social Security kicked in. By this time my back with all its injuries just about brought me to a stop. I applied for a disability but since I was not injured on a job my application was refused. My grandmother had always told me there was always a way, you just had to find it. I always believed her and her saying has always worked for me. Since I've been here I have raised calves, sheep, goats, horses, cows, pigs and poultry. You'd think I was back on the ranch. I just have a small acreage.

During this retirement time I found I inherited some of my mother's artistic talents and have filled my extra time painting pictures for my friends and a couple of huge fantastic murals. I still paint when the mood strikes me no and then. The following photo is of one of my Murals that was quite a challenge.

When I sit out under my trees and watch our New Mexico sunsets, I might do a little sketch for later when I have more time . . .

This is the side of a Las Cruces feed store

My great grandchildren have been a joy for me as they joined Four H and are doing well. But from time to time, they had to come home and live with me.

One day I wandered into a small church called Wellspring. I thought I had found the spot I had been searching for all my life. I found friendship, love, acceptance and encouragement and appreciation for who I truly am. What more can I say or wish. I have love, and contentment of my family and friends, and am able to enjoy the shade and beauty of my yard which are the fruits of my labor. I feel I have led a pretty wonderful life and so it is.

This is Gale Reciting a poem at Wellspring Church 2008

. . .

GRANDMOTHER MARY

As I have mentioned before, Grandma did not seem very affectionate to anyone including Dale who was her pride and joy. She did take real good care of all of us. As I mentioned earlier, Grandmother Mary, because of her training back in Kansas, and the lack if medical help, she became the Caring Angel of Sulfur Springs Valley. People would come in wagons, buggies and horseback to get her to come and take care of their sick family members. She never turned any of them down.

I can remember thinking of her a being crippled. She had tripped over one of Dale's little wagons and threw her hip out of place. It was never put back in place.

Though we were very poor, she would make beautiful things with whatever she had to work with, be it rocks or her house plants. She always wanted to be first in the Valley. We had the first up-town bathroom but she would not let mother put the toilet in the house because she felt it would smell. She had them build little house out back to house the darn contraption. It wasn't long before she made us all go back to the out-house because she felt the toilet took too much water and she needed to save the water for her cattle.

We had the first carbide light in the valley. Grandmother had a party to show off our new gadgets. When the party was over, it was back to the coal oil lamps.

Grandmother was a very frugal person, and now I realize that she had to make every penny count in order to keep us all fed. However, I remember that during the depression, she took in three whole families and took care of all of us.

Dale had farmed forty acres of pinto beans and had a great crop. We also had a milk cow for dairy products, chickens and the cotton tailed rabbits were thick as fleas. She felt that with milk, butter, eggs, beans and meat we wouldn't go hungry.

Grandmother and Grandfather were always fussing or arguing. After Grandfather passed on, Grandmother said, "You know, I don't know why I didn't realize what a good man Charlie was. He was always good to our girls. He never raised a hand to me and I made him miserable fussing at him because he wasn't as ambitious as I though he ought to be. Now that he is gone, I realize how much he really did."

After losing Grandfather Rathbun, we took turns staying with Grandmother Mary

Pecos ran out of a job and came home and stayed with her almost a year—he wasn't drinking as neither he nor Grandmother knew how to drive so they had to send out for supplies. Pecos thought a lot of her and was really very good to her during those hard times.

Then, one fine day, Dale came home and took both of them to town and Pecos picked up a jug. All bets were off and it was time for him to move on.

CGee and I came home from Louisiana for a vacation and ended up staying for about four months. By this time, Bernice was ready to come to the Ranch and take over.

After she had been there for about three years, it was Mabel's turn, but she would not come unless Grandmother signed the Ranch over to her. Now Grandmother Mary was 88 years old, she was still sharp and told her the property belonged to Bernice because she had give Mabel her Grandfather's place, she would not give her the Ranch. In the end she did sign over 10 acres where the house stood. As you might imagine, this affected the entire family as we all felt that the old place would be our home til the end of time. All of us had to move the stuff we had stored there.

This arrangement continued for about two years when Aunt Mabel told us she couldn't take care of Grandmother any longer. By this time, Bernice had her home in Cochise and Grandmother was moved there. Both girls took care of her until she died.

Then, because Mabel's friends Hazel and Tom had bought lots in Cochise, she decided to build on half the lots. She went back to work at Riggs and turned the building plans over to Bernice. Bernice was in her glory as she because she didn't have to do it all herself, she could boss the job.

Around this time Buck and Gale returned home from California and Buck was able to hire on as a helper so the house went up in a hurry.

Introduction to short stories

The following short stories are an elaboration of the family and friends in my life's story. I wanted to put some "flesh" on these characters so you'd see them as I did. I may repeat myself but that happens when you put flesh on bare bones. I hope I did them justice . . .

MABLE RATHBUN-CONROY

I HAVEN'T WRITTEN MUCH ABOUT Aunt Mable, known as Aunty to me. She was working for Ed and Lillian Riggs at the Faraway Ranch when uncle Mart died. Shortly after that, the Faraway Ranch became a Private Boys School. At this time, Mable was able to bring her son Tom up with her to the Private Boys School.

He became fast friends with the boys who were there. But Ed's son Marray was his special pal. Ed also had a daughter who in later life married the Author Dean Stratten Porter..

Mable was given the job of House Mother in addition to being the School Cook. She became "Mother" to all of the boys. And with her loving personality, it wasn't very long before the new boys who came there felt the same way about her.

They were mostly boys from wealthy families who wanted them to experience the real wild-west.

One of the boys, Curtis Cooper, fell in love with the country and convinced his family to come out and look over the country.

I have written before about the Rancho Manzanita that Mrs. Ainsworth built. It had twelve guest room with baths, full dining room with a huge living area along with adjoining room with several pool tables. An Olympic size swimming pool and tennis courts.

Lilian (Mrs. Riggs) was ready to close the boy's school when Curtis convinced his folks to buy the ranch and continue the school. His father, Calvin C. Cooper had been President of the General Motors Corp. back in New York and was ready to retire. Mr. Cooper found that he also loved the Arizona country as much as his son. The deal was made. And Mable and Mr. Sours, the Tutor, came with the deal.

Those were happy years for Mable and the boys. Most of the boys were ready to go on to College so Mr. Cooper turned the Boys School into a Guest Ranch for his wealthy friends.

While there, Mable met and made many true friends who still came to visit her after she retired and had a home of her own. When Mable was able to quit work and draw SS, Bernice had the Cochise house ready for her to put on the finishing touches.

She had made curtains made out of thickly starched Burlap that had been appliquéd with red and black material. This was all done in Indian design language. When they were put up on the windows, and back lit by the sun, they told a story of a young buck who had been out hunting and found the maiden of his dreams. He loaded her and her belongings on her horse and they rode to the big mountains where there was plenty of game to keep them in meat he rest of their lives. There, they threw up their teepee, raised their family and lived happily ever after.

Grandmother's Rock Wall

I had live at the Old ranch House before her home was built and knew she was going to need all her friendship rocks. So I chiseled the rocks out of the fireplace wall. The was going to be the rocks third move. The fireplace in the Cochise house took up the entire north wall. She designed the fireplace with stair steps so she would have places to put her favorite cactus plants. Aunt Mable took the rocks and inserted them all over the wall. The most impressive thing about these rocks was the simple fact that she could tell you a story of their origin and who gave them to her.

Many of her boys in the service had gathered special rocks when they were over seas and sent the home to her. This fireplace has been quite often photographed and featured in local magazines.

Her bathroom was also a place of interest. Sometime in her life, she had seen a cartoon of some little boys swimming nude in a pond, and visualized this scene as a mural behind the tub. With the help of her sister Bernice, who was an artist, and a friend, that did art profiles, it

came to life much as she visualized it.

Bathtub Mural

The outside yard was decorated in rock formations much like her mother, Mary Rathbun, had built at the Home ranch. She had a lily pond rock walkway. Her bird baths were made from Indian matates. This last home gave Aunt Mable a lot of challenge in her creative endeavors. She was extremely proud to have all her friends visit her there.

Aunt Mable was my favorite Aunt . . .

AUNT MABLE

Mabel was hired on as a cook at the Faraway Ranch. Mr. Sours, one of the teachers, invited Tom to come down to Bisbee and stay with their family until he finished High School.

The next year Tom graduated from High School and entered the University of Arizona. While there, he worked two jobs to pay his way. This was Aunt Mabel's dream and it continued on until he graduated from college.

Aunt Mabel had an opportunity to buy some acreage Northwest of Douglas where she started a chicken farm. Tom was now in the Army Air Corps and was able to help her a little.

WWII started about this time. Mabel was able to rent out trailer spaces all this time she was building her little adobe home with Bernice's help. She went in with her neighbor and started Saturday night dances. for extra income. I lived with her during this time as well as working at the airport.

It was in this home that she built her first "friendship fireplace." All her friends would bring her a pretty rocks or Indian Arrows. Anything something special, she would stick it in the wall of her fireplace. When the boys were over seas, they would also send her something special and she would add them to the fireplace.

After the war was over, Tom met his special girl and invited Aunt Mabel back east for their wedding.

During her time at the Guest Ranch, she made many friends who insisted that if she ever got back east, she had to spend some time with each of them. She was visiting with the Rosenfields when we lost Grandfather Charles. It just wasn't feasible for her to attend the funeral because they were having it the following day. Mrs. Rosenfield was a very strong Christian Scientist which was Auntie's Religion of choice. She helped Auntie through her grief period.

After losing Grandfather, we each took turns staying with Grandmother Mary. She couldn't drive and was quite crippled. My mother took the first couple of years, then Pecos had returned to the valley and helped.

I had come home and stayed for about three months. When Pecos went back to the White Mountains, Bernice came back but told Mabel she didn't have enough money to stay without working and by this time Grandmother had cut down the size of her herd. Mabel said she would sell her place and just move home if Grandmother would give her the Ranch

When Grandfather Charles died, Grandmother Mary deeded his place, and acreage, that my father had turned over to him, to Aunt Mabel. Bernice said all she ever wanted was the home place she had traded her homestead for. This gave Mabel Grandpa's homestead, the James Quarter Section that Chy had proved up on, and her original homestead.

Grandmother Mary said she felt that was Mabel's share and would not deed Bernice's property back to her. This created a break in family relations. Bernice told Grandmother to deed the 10 acres with the Ranch house to Mabel. She felt we could all share the Ranch house if we were in need as we always had in the days past.

This seemed to work for us until Aunt Mabel and brother Dale got cross ways. Aunt Mabel told Dale move his cattle and possessions from the Ranch. Dale Gave Bernice a deed to the place he bought in Cochise so she could start another home place. This worked for all of us.

While Mabel was at the Ranch she missed her fireplace. When she sold out in Douglas, she chiseled out her friendship rocks and then replaced them with turquoise and minerals.

At this time the Ranch house had two bedrooms upstairs over the ground floor and a sleeping porch. Aunt Mabel knocked out a doorway in the adobe wall and added a new room, a beautiful big window facing the sunsets over the Cochise Stronghold and a new fireplace.

Grandmother loved this room and she spent most of her time there.

This arrangement went on until Aunt Mabel was bitten by a Rattlesnake on an excursion to the Chiricahua Mountains. Her friends rushed her home and Grandmother got busy with her using Lye water soak because it took them 40 minutes to get her home and her leg was terribly swollen.

It took Mabel a long time to heal so it was decided that since Bernice had finished her home in Cochise, Grandmother would go there to be with her.

In the mean time, Mabel's best friends down through the years, Tom & Hazel Bundy, had made a visit to Cochise. They fell in love with that area and decided to buy there and retire. Together with Mabel, they were able to buy a very large lot and divided it. Tom began working on their home and Mabel went back to work at the John Riggs Ranch to save for her new home. The Ranch House at home was empty.

Bernice had cared for Grandmother who was becoming very frail. It wasn't long before Mabel had to come home to Cochise to help with her care.

Bernice & Mabel in 1956

Tommy Conroy and his family were being transferred to Japan and Tom wanted his mother to come with them. Mabel declined the offer because she couldn't let Bernice carry the whole load.

After we lost Grandmother Mary at the tender age of 94, Mabel went back to work at the Riggs Ranch. She left the construction of her new home place to Bernice to oversee. As I said earlier, Bernice was in her glory because building was her passion. She managed the subcontractors and loved that part of the job. As you may have guessed by now, the new home place had to have a new Friendship fireplace.

All this was going on when my present husband, Buck, had moved to the old Home Ranch to live. I spent the winter chiseling those Friendship rocks out of the fireplace for Aunt Mabel to re-install in her new fireplace in Cochise.

Aunt Mabel had an amazing memory. She could name each of those rocks and tell the story that went along with it. She could tell the best stories about the old days and times.

After she was able to retire, she came home to her finished house. She decided it was time to landscape the place. The end result was beautiful. Her last days there were quite full and happy til Tom Bundy was killed in a car crash.

Her best friend Hazel moved away and it was around this time that Aunt Mabel's son Tom died when his plane blew up over Japan. A short time later My mother, Bernice, passed away and I'm sure she felt life was not worth it anymore. Although she had many friends, Aunt Mabel felt she had lost nearly all of her family. Dale and I were the only close ones left. I went home to take care of her in the last days. Her attorney finally made her go into the hospital, not for medicine but for nursing care. I was having severe back problems and he felt I couldn't take proper care of her.

She only lasted ten days in the hospital. Her grand daughters flew up to be with her. She was never left alone there and Aunt Mabel never lost her sense of humor.

One night when my Nieces Cristin, and Cathy was sitting with Mabel, she started singing "Among My Souvenirs." Both girls had heard that song before and came out of the room crying thinking Mabel was delirious.

One thing I do remember sitting up with her when she said, "You know Gale, you mother was in all ways better at everything I ever did. She was a better builder, cooking, and art. Any thing I could think up, she could do better than me all of our lives. The one thing I did beat her at was outliving her for a year and ten days."

Mabel had even figured out the time to the exact day. I tried to tell her their talents were for different things. Mother wasn't very sociable although you could count her truly good friends on two hands. Auntie Mabel had hundreds of people that loved her. Mother's creative art was in landscaping, Auntie's art subjects were animals, and she was much more creative than my mother.

I told her that it took the two of them together to make such a great team! I also told her that when they were together again they would re-join to make a happy team. About an hour later she was gone . . . She was a great gal and I loved her.

DALE'S STORIES

Dale in Cochise, AZ approximately 1976.

WHEN DALE GRADUATED THE eighth grade he was very grown up and mature. He would have loved to have gone on to high school and played baseball, but he realized what an expense it would have been to his Grandmother, so he told her he didn't want to go and he was going to work. He had been the area's mechanic and extra cowboy. The nearest neighbor, Jay Pressy, was an avid hunter and loved to have Dale with him because Dale was a dead shot. Dale's Aunt Mabel went to work for Harry Kendall at the Guest Ranch near Tombstone. She talked Harry into hiring Dale to wrangle his dudes. Dale had a fine line of stories about riding and hunting that they all loved.

He got a job one summer with the Forest Service as a lookout. Later, he became interested in mining. He and a friend, Lee West, got a job lowering a well in Texas Canyon where it was very rocky and they had to do a lot of blasting with dynamite. One night they drilled out their holes, filled them with sticks of dynamite and they always shot at night so the air and fumes would have receded by morning. Then they had to go down and clean out the loose muck. This time not all the sticks had fired, but they thought by morning it would be OK. When Dale went down to send out the muck, he turned on the air hose to blow out the stale air, five sticks of dynamite ignited and he was blown to the top. Lee said had he been in position he could have caught him. As it was he fell back in with all the muck on top of him. When they dug him out and took him to the hospital they found he had a broken back along with a lot of rock pounded into his body. He was extremely lucky to have survived.

The hospital put him into a body cast that had him all bent over. When they found out he was just a poor kid and was not working for a big mining company, they realized they would have trouble getting their money, they just let him go home. Grandmother said the way they had made the cast, Dale would have been a cripple all bent over, so she cut it off, put him into an old fashioned stayed corset and put boards under his bed so he could heal up straight as an arrow. Lee had been trained as a chiropractor and kept him adjusted and straight so when he was checked out after he was drafted into the Army, Dale asked them why they took so many x-rays and they told him the last three were trying to find out how he could walk with an injury like that. Lee had a daughter named Thelma who had caught Dale's eye and he had dated now and then during those days.

While he was recuperating he went to work as a watch man at the Coronado Mine. There he met and old mining engineer, Mr. Wright who took a real interest in him and hired him. Later Dale was to become a hoist engineer. Dale had talked his cousin, Tom Conroy, into taking mining engineering at the University of Arizona because Dale thought between the two of them, they might really do some good. The war came along and since Tom had taken ROTC, he was called to service and he had an unplanned career change.

During this time, Dale and Thelma were married and he went to work for the Douglas Airport.

Dale vs. Deer

"Dale, how did you get him off the rope?"

Above pictures of Dale roping a deer

It was at this time that I also went to work at the airport as a teletype and Western Union Operator. It was there that I met my future husband Pete Ginn. He had made the first three point landing and was supposed to be the best pilot in his class so I asked my girlfriend, DeBee Dearing, who sang for the USO, to introduce me and the rest is history. When he was shipped to Washington State he would call me every night at work and beg me to come up to Washington. I finally weakened and we were finally married in Spokane in 1943.

We lived for a while in Lewiston, Montana before he was shipped overseas to England. Pete was a B-17 pilot who had been shot down three times and still made it back to his wife and little daughter CGee.

When I came home pregnant, Thelma told Dale she wanted a baby too. Cathy was about a year and three months behind my daughter. Tommy Conroy waited until he got home to marry a girl he met overseas who was Gen. Kepner's secretary. They had two girls, Cristin and Connie.

MARVIN 'CHEYANNE' CHAMBERLAIN

I KNOW I MENTIONED EARLIER how 'Chy' came into the picture of our family but I feel I need a little more time to make you know how truly important he became to me much later in my life. My first true memory of him must have been when I was about three years old. I'm dating this on the fact the Mother and Aunt Mable had not added on to the Buckwater two-story house. (We later referred to it as the home-place.)

One evening I remember Grandpa saying; "Mom, I saw car lights turn down at the Mont Boots Corner (This was another homestead). I guess they are planning on coming over to play cards again tonight." Grandmother grabbed my hand and we started upstairs to bed. She told Grandpa to tell them we'd already gone to bed. She told us the only reason they came up, was to be comfortable using our wood and lamp oil. You see, my grandmother was very frugal and watched every penny.

It wasn't long until Grandpa called upstairs and said, "Mom, bring Gale down, its Gale's father and he has come this evening to see her." I don't remember much of the evening but remembering Grandpa and Chy bringing in a lot of stuff. Chy had brought a hundred pounds of flour, a large sack of sugar, beans and corn and several cans of shortening or lard in 10 gallon pails. I remember seeing them stacked up against the wall. There was a big box of something else, but of course the only thing I really remember, was that he brought me a little washboard and a lot of candy.

When I was in the first grade at Ash Creek, he came out of Mexico and went to the Manzaneta Ranch (Which is now the El Coronado) and picked up my mother and then came down and got me out of school. I have often wondered if he came out of Mexico to get my mother to go back with him, but it didn't work.

When I was in the White Mountains around the age of 10, I asked my mother about him. She would never tell me much except she didn't want me raised in Mexico.

When I was going to high school in Pearce, Gladys McCloud had heard about our family from her mother, Mrs. Huddy. Gladys was the postmistress and had received a letter for Chy. Even though I was using the name of Higgins instead of Chamberlain, she gave the letter to me. It was from an old Army friend of his who needed him to verify something so he could get his pension and was hoping to locate him.

Somehow when I was changing classes I dropped the letter. Tom Gillespie in my class saw me drop the letter, and when he picked it up and saw who it was addressed to, he asked me who

Chy was. He told me his father had just come out of Mexico and had told stories of staying with Chy when he was there. One day at school I was called into the office and told I had a message that my Dad and he would be in Douglas at my Aunt's. I was to come down with the mail carrier.

My boyfriend, Bunt Wooten had a stripped down car (That was a car without a windshield, top or anything, just seats on the frame) and volunteered to take me. When I got there, I was told Chy's sisters had been trying to find him. They had written to the Army who told them if they would send him a letter, via the Army, they in turn would send it to him. If he wanted to reply it would be up to him. Chy had arranged to meet in Douglas, however, his sisters had to leave before I got there. I never did meet them until after WWII.

Chy had come out of Mexico during the war and bought a little house in Douglas and went to work on the railroad train from Douglas to El Paso taking care of the mail. After the war he went to work as a line rider for the Border Patrol. He still maintained his ranch in Mexico along with a Mexican wife, Tita. Back in those days it was frowned upon to inter-marry, however I thought Tita was a very nice woman who dearly loved Chy and took very good care of him.

When I left Louisiana, CGee and I were living with my Aunt in Douglas, AZ. This is when Chy bought a beautiful little Mexican sorrel horse for CGee to ride. How she loved that pony and we named him Seabee. She was to ride him for at least 10 years until we left the country and retired him rather than sell him.

Dale had brought over to the home ranch an old sorrel horse named Satan. He was a big old horse, would not hurt a child, but he did step on CGee's toe once. She was screaming, and I ran out of the house and the horse didn't know what was wrong and was rubbing her head with his nose to soothe her. This was her first horse. Once when I had driven to Douglas for supplies, Mother had led Satan down to the Boots Corner. I came along about then so Mother put the reins around Satan's neck, turned him around and told him to take CGee home. Then she got into the car and we followed them; her first solo ride when she was two.

When we were flying home to Louisiana over the middle of New Mexico, CGee called the stewardess and said, "Tell the pilot to stop and let me out, I have decided to go back and live with my horse".

While I was living in Douglas, I was working for Hannigans Dairy and the Paramount Movie Company came to make a movie called 'Branded'. They needed a girl who could ride well to do the rough riding for the star, Mona Freeman. The dairy donated me for publicity. Now Pecos did make a whale of a bronc rider out of me, but he had not taught me any of the finer points of riding, just survival and endurance. During this time I had the chance to spend more time with Chy who was known as a great horseman. He new all the finer points of riding, and I found out he had won his nickname "Cheyenne' by riding in the rodeo and winning the bareback championship in Cheyenne, Wyoming with a curry comb on one foot and a brush on the other instead of spurs.

He never was much to tell me about his life when he was a boy except that his father was a Methodist minister. He had a little sister, Lena who would go home and tattle on him when he got a whipping in school. His dad would then give him another one. He had left the North Country (Nebraska area) and had joined the cavalry in WWI. When the Border Patrol relocated him to Lochiel he asked if I would like his Douglas house. I told him I would love it if he would let me remodel it, and I did.

Chy joined the Sheriffs Posse and was also a member of the Elks Club and American Legion. During his last years when he was about 65, he became a pilot. His excuse was that the roads were to rough to his Mexico ranch. He also joined a polo club in Tucson. When I asked him if he thought 80 was a little old for the game his reply was "they may be better than me but I have a better horse". He died after being successful on a deer hunt, and was buried in Douglas, Arizona

TOMMY CONROY

TOMMY CONROY WENT TO live at the Faraway Ranch when his mother, Mabel, was the Ranch Cook and House Mother for the Dude boys. These boys were there at the Boys School.

While there Tom became lifelong friends with the Ranch owners' son Murray Riggs.

We still have deer head they sent to a taxidermist. Tom said he and Murray were hunting and both shot at the same time and both hit him. Naturally both boy claimed it was his shot that put him down.

After the Faraway Ranch decided to close the Boys School, one of the boys fathers bout up the Guest Ranch, The Mannita and re-named it The El Coronado and started another Boys School. It was here that Tom made friends with several influential people.

Tom's mother was hired in the same capacity as cook and house mother. Tom stayed there until they also closed the Boys School. Then Tom went down to Bisbee and boarded with one of his Teachers, Mr. Sours until he graduated from High School..

His mother was adamant for Tom to get an education and saved every penny for his college tuitions. Tom taught Ball Room Dancing, worked in a cafeteria, and other odd jobs during this time. He and my brother Dale always palled around together in the summer at the Ranch.

Dale was very interested in mining and talked Tom into getting a Mining Engineering Degree. Tom was also in ROTC during this time.

The summer he graduated, he met a Mr. Dean who was President of Genera Motors Corp. He liked Tom and told him if he would go to work for his company, he would give him a chance to go all the way to the to top as quickly as his talents and ability would take him.

Mr. Dean's wife had been out to the Dude Ranch and was the one who wrote the story of my trip and sent it to Reg Manning of the Phoenix Republican Gazette newspaper.

Mr. Dean placed Tommy in the GM Seattle Company because tom thought being raised in the west, he would like Seattle better than New York City where Mr. Dean lived.

In 1941, Tom was called to active duty in the Army due to his ROTC status. A friend of his from the El Coronado School, Walter Rosenfield, talked Tom into going into the Army Air Corps and become a pilot. During the war, Tom became a B-24 pilot and was sent to the European Theater stationed in England. It was at this time that he met his wife to be, a girl from Pennsylvania. She was the secretary to General Kempner.

Tommy used to kid that Val would not know how to go to the bathroom if she didn't have the facilities. There just wasn't anything in the book of current events that she didn't know and she was a great help to him in climbing the ladder to succeed in the Air Corps. He was sent to the Army War College, served in the Pentagon and then was sent to Massiura, Japan as Commander of the Air Field there.

Tommy and Val had two daughters, Cristin Gay and Connie Lou Conway about this time. While in Japan they were told there was going to b an Air Force Air Show. The family was told that Tom took out what I believe was a F-86 Saber Jet to get extra flying hours and experience flying it. This happened on a Sunday. Tom and a friend, who had more experience flying in formation than Tom did, decided to practice for the upcoming Air Show.

They took off in formation and Tommy began in familiarization with his friend walking him through the various maneuvers.

Tommy was just three minutes from the field when he radioed, "I have a flame out, am ejecting." His friend told him his best chance was to crash land on the beach. The accident report stated that he was just a quarter mile short when it blew up with Tommy aboard.

Val and Tom had already started their home in Florida so she brought the children back there to raise them at Shalimar.

We never had a chance to get to know them very well until both girls grew up and re-located to California.

The following story is a very interesting glimpse into Tommy's experience during WWII in Europe:

One of the strange stories that came out after WWII went something like this: My husband Pete Ginn had joined the Army and was a Medic because he had not attended college. Sometime in late 1942, the Army was short of pilots so if any of the boys could pass a series of tests, they let them join the Air Corps and trained them to be pilots.

Pete became a B-17 pilot and was sent overseas in the early spring of 1943. I also had a cousin Tommy Conroy who was in the Air Corps. He was a B-24 pilot. All during the war these two had never met because they were assigned to different Squadrons in different parts of England.

They both were lucky enough to make it back home, and they met for the first time back on our old ranch sitting out on the land bank under the shade of an apple tree sharing a cold beer. Like many veteran pilots, they were discussing different missions when Tom made a remark about a certain mission and an accident he had witnessed. Pete asked him what the mission was and Tom told Pete what the mission target and date had been. A surprised Pete told Tom he had been on that same mission. Tom went on to describe seeing a plane get a direct hit and as it went down, it hit this other bomber and sheared the whole tail section off.

Tom said that old boy flying it, turned her around and headed back for England. He went on to reminisce that he often wondered if they made it back to base. Now here is where it gets strange—it was Pete's aircraft that lost the tail. Pete just grinned a bit and said, "Yeah, we made it after being picked up in the North Sea after freezing for ten hours.

Pete had also shot down over North Africa just for practice . . .

When Pete was ordered back to the states for B-29 training he knew he was going to be sent to the Pacific theater. As I wrote before, Pete was high point man because of his accumulated mission hours, Distinguished Fling Medal, Air Medal, Silver Star, and the Soldiers Medial for saving a soldier life with his medical training. After soul searching and considering his flying experiences in Europe, Pete requested and was granted a discharge just before Japan surrendered.

Sometimes war stories really are stranger than fiction . . .

THE RANCH

The old Ranch House

THIS PLACE WAS GENERALLY known as the "Ranch," a homestead proved up on by the Buckwalters in 1909. When

Bernice and Pecos split the blanket, Bernice traded her Happy Hollow homestead to her neighbor Mattie Pressy for the Buckwalters. The Buckwalters placed joined her father and sister Mable's homestead. It also had a two story lumber house on the property and it was a little closer to haul water from Grandpa's place.

Bernice knew she would have to go back to work and Grandmother, who had claimed Dale as her own, would need a better place to live. Grandmother who was the most wonderful manager in the world on little or nothing traded out work to get a well dug on the place. A few years later, Bernice was not working one summer, and she built on an adobe addition, which was a kitchen, dinette, bathroom, two bedrooms, a sleeping porch and a front porch. Grandmother said she was never satisfied, so she cut a hole in the roof and put in a sweeping out window set she had seen in a magazine giving the upstairs more light and ventilation. It didn't leak either.

Dale, Tommy Conroy and Gale pretty much grew up here as both Bernice and Mable had to go back to work to keep the ranch going. By this time Grandmother Mary had acquired cows, horses, chickens and there was a little irrigation ditch leading from Turkey Creek by the house that she could irrigate a little garden. Dale, at 14, put in 40 acres of pinto beans and corn.

The picture in the next page was taken by Tommy Conroy from an airplane back in 1946. If you use a magnifying glass, you can see Grandmother's rock work in the front of the ranch house near the top. If you look close near the upper tree, you should be able to spot the Elevated tank and the windmill. As you can see from the following photo, the Home Ranch was a pretty big ranch

The shadows in the foreground were from our cattle herd.

An aerial view of the ranch taken by Tommy Conroy

During the depression Grandmother took in three different families who had lost everything. She had milk, eggs, butter and Dale would hunt for cottontail rabbits to help feed the families. We also had a pond stocked with little mud catfish, which was always a treat. We learned to love frog legs as well.

Bernice decided to put up an elevated water tank. She built the forms and then everyone hunted up all the old steel and iron and wire and everything that would hold cement together. She would put about four feet at a time. Years later we used to muse over the fact that in the dark of the moon, the seams would dry but when the moon changed the seams on the tank would seep a little water. We surely had water pressure in the house after she got it plumbed. She even piped water out to the corrals and when the wind was strong it would fill the pond where we had the catfish. After a few years Grandmother's cattle herd grew so there was more need for water.

Then she started making her place more attractive with rockwork. Grandfather Rathbun would hitch up the team and we would go to Turkey Creek and Ash Creek for sand and rock. When Bernice had added on the bathroom, Grandmother made her build a little house outside for the flush toilet. She was afraid it would smell. Ours was the first bathroom of its kind in the Valley. Grandmother soon found the flush toilet took too much water and we had to return to the old outhouse.

As I have stated before, Grandmother did not seem very affectionate, even to Dale who was her pride and joy, but she did take real good care of us.

As I have mentioned before, due to her training back in Kansas and the lack of medical help she became the caring angel of Sulfur Springs Valley. People would come in wagons or buggies to get her to take care of their sick families and she would never turn them down. I can always remember thinking she was very crippled. She had tripped over one of Dale's little wagons and had thrown her hip out of place and it was never put back properly.

She always wanted to be first with everything. After the bathroom came the first carbide light in the Valley. We had one giant party to show off our new light, then back to the coal oil lamps. Grandmother and Grandfather were always fussing or arguing but after we lost Grandpa Grandma said "You know I don't know why I didn't realize what a good man Charlie was. He was always good to our girls, never raised a hand to me and I made him miserable fussing at him because he wasn't as ambitious as I thought he should be. Now that he is gone, I truly realized all that he did." After loosing Grandpa, the family took turns staying with her. Pecos had run out of a job and stayed with her for almost a year. He wasn't drinking and neither he nor Grandmother drove and had to send for supplies. Pecos thought a lot of her and was very good to her. One day Dale came home and took both of them to town. Pecos got a jug and all bets were off; it was time for him to go.

CGee and Gale came home from Louisiana for a vacation and ended up staying for about four months. By this time, Bernice was ready to come home to the ranch and take over. After Bernice had been there for about three years it was Mable's turn, but she would not come unless Grandmother would sign the ranch over to her.

Grandmother was about 88 years old and still sharp and told Mable it originally belonged to Bernice and since she had given Mable her Grandfathers place she would not do that. The outcome was she signed over about 10 acres where the house stood. This affected the whole family as we had felt the Old Place would be our home until the end of time and we all had to move our stuff we had stored there.

This arrangement continues for about two years and then Mable said she couldn't take care of Grandmother any more. By this time Bernice had her home built in Cochise, Arizona, and they brought Grandmother up there where she was cared for until she died.

Then, because Mable's friends, Hazel and Tom Bundy had bought lots in Cochise, she also bought lots and decided to build on half of her lots. She went back to work at Riggs's Ranch and turned her building plans over to Bernice who was in her glory because she didn't have to do it all herself and could boss the job. At this time Buck (Gale's new Husband) and Gale had come home from California. Buck was hired as a helper and Mable's house went up in a hurry.

Story Of The Round Elevated Tank

ONE PARTICULAR MORNING I woke up remembering it was Dela's birthday. Dela is the daughter of Cathy who was the daughter of Dale and Thelma. She turned 30 today, and add 43 more years and you would kind of know how old I am feeling. Realizing that if I am going to tell our kids some of the stories that happened in my lifetime I had better get busy.

I am not sure what brought our Old Elevated Tank into mind, unless it was the city putting in a water line beside my property. I was only about four years old when mother (Bernice) and Grandmother Mary had figured out how to build an elevated tank. Grandpa Charles hooked up old Bessy and Blue and rode over to Ash Creek, Arizona to haul a load of sand for the cement. Bernice had Dale picking up any old wire and iron that would fit into six-inch wide frames made from wagon wheel rims. She would pour the cement in for about four feet high at a time then she would leave the iron and wire in a rough top so it would adhere to the next level. She added more levels until it was almost 20 feet high. The tank, as I remembered, was about 10 feet across and I am sure she got her ideas from the grain silos that the Kansas people who homesteaded out here built. Anyway, it was a wonderful tank, and we had great water storage and great water pressure inside the house. Our only water supply at that time came from a windmill.

Then Dale and Grandpa got an old hand scraper, hitched up old Bessy and Blue and built a dirt tank that Dale stocked with catfish. They built a little bridge out into the tank and Grandmother used to go out and call the fish and feed them the leavings of the dough when she was making bread.

When mother built this tank she must not have thought ahead as to how to clean it. She had a bottom drain but the only way to clean it was to put a ladder down and scrub it with a brush and bail out the moss. Needless to say it didn't get scrubbed and cleaned too often. On day, Dale and his wife Thelma came over to clean it for Grandma. I was lucky enough to capture them on my trusty Brownie camera when they were through and needless to say the pictures were gorgeous.

Once when Buck Moorhead, daughter CGee, and I were living there, they decided to clean the tank. Buck sent CGee down on a rope instead of a ladder and told her, he would be back later. That was his way of teasing her. Then he was afraid that she would be so mad she'd half kill him if she did get out. I finally went out and put the ladder down to her. CGee was patient and just waited for the right time so she could truly even the score. Buck said he couldn't be mad because he knew he deserved it. CGee and Sonny (Buck's son) tied hard their lariats to Buck's jeep. The jeep didn't have any brakes, so when they went through the corral gate, those kids roped a post and bailed off the jeep. When the jeep hit the end of the rope, it launched Buck over the front end . . .

THE RUNAWAY WAGON

ONCE WHEN I WAS about 5 years old, I talked Grandpa into letting me ride with him on the high spring seat of the old work wagon. We went over to Ash Creek and Grandfather loaded the bed with sand and then we started up the old creek that was filled with big Sacaton grass.

Something jumped up in the grass, maybe a jackrabbit, but anyway it scared the team, Bessy and Blue. They broke into a run in that rough terrain. Grandpa was afraid I was going to get hurt so he picked out a big bunch of Sacaton and pitched me into the middle of it.

Sacaton has long narrow sharp blades and one of them split the tip of my nose. Grandpa wasn't as lucky as me. The team turned the wagon over, ran over him and broke some ribs.

He had to walk to the neighbors for help to get the wagon back on its wheels. On the way back they found this poor little kid walking back crying. When Grandpa saw my bloody nose, I learned some new words. Of course I didn't know they were cuss words at the time – yeah sure.

This is one of the incidences I remember so well.

Nora And Tom

ONE AFTERNOON I GOT into a bunch of old letters that reminded me of many stories of our nearest neighbors, Nora and Tom Stafford; they were truly characters. Nora was a very good friend of my mothers and I had just finished reading a birthday letter she had written to me on my 40th birthday telling about how she had loaded up in their old Model T Ford to make the trip to Douglas over washboard roads to see me when I was born.

Tom & Nora Stafford

Nora said Mother was still in bed. When I was growing up with Grandma and Grandpa, Nora and Tom would come over to play Pitch. Tom and Grandpa used to play partners, and Nora would accuse them of cheating and throw the cards all over table. Nora had a fabulous memory for birthdays, and I don't think she ever forgot one if she knew them. One summer, Tom built a new fence between his place and ours. The rains had been spotty, but there was thunderstorm rolling in. It rained on Tom's place up to the fence he had built and then quit. Grandmother said she was going to tear his damn fence down so the rain could get through the next time.

I was in high school, but I had been visiting Dale at the Coronado Mines near Dragoon, Arizona during the summer. The Webb Rodeo and Dance was coming up and Nora and Tom told me I could go with them. I took off pretty early on horseback and it was about 36 miles to Grandmother Mary's Ranch. That afternoon a terrible dust storm blew up. I had to stop with a family named Grace in the Kansas Settlement. When the rain came and settled the dust, I started on for about 15 miles. The night got real black except for the lightening and it was slow going but I could see the Chiricahuas in the flashes. I got home about 2:00 am in the morning and put up my horse and went in the house. Grandmother, being a light sleeper came out to see about the noise. When she had found out that I had ridden through that storm, she really 'blessed' my brother Dale out. She was not going to let me go to the rodeo but Nora and Tom talked her into it. That was a big time in my life.

SOME OF GRANDMOTHER'S MEDICAL RECIPES

ANOTHER EVENING, A GOOD friend named Sarah phoned, and in conversation I was telling her about old fashioned remedies my Grandmother used when she was treating people in the Sulpher Springs Valley. There was a doctor in Willcox about 30 miles north of us and the next nearest was in Douglas or Bisbee about 60 miles to the south. Folks between the Chiricahua Mountains and the Stronghold brought their problems to her. I've long forgotten how many babies in the Valley she was midwife for. She would meet them later and say, "Did you know, you are one of my babies?"

During the flu epidemic of 1919, she had her husband and one daughter so people would come to get her as she didn't drive. I asked her what she did back in those days and she said her standard treatment was to give them a hot mustard footbath with a hot toddy then a mustard wrap poultice on the chest and back. Then put them to bed with a big shot of Castor Oil. She said the treatment above usually broke the fever and the secret was keeping them warm, and the Castor Oil carried away the body's impurities. She added that in some cases, she used a bread and milk poultice to the throat and chest.

I asked her what she did to keep from getting the flu herself. She told me she would take a spoonful of Cream of Tartar every morning in a full glass of water. She used this as a blood purifier to fight off the germs.

She had two standard remedies for snakebite or blood poisoning. This was bathing or soaking the bite in hot lye water. Afterwards, she would wash the wound with clear water and rub it with butter to kill the lye. If she could not soak it, she would make hot cow poultices (sic) to apply until she could draw out the poison and follow that with Castor Oil.

Oh, how I hated Castor Oil, but she claimed it cleaned your whole system.

For my ear aches, she would wrap a bit of black pepper in cotton, dip it in sweet oil, and have my Grandfather blow my ear full of warm smoke, insert the cotton, and place a hot water bottle over the ear. It always seemed to work.

My brother Dale got very badly burned by gasoline. Once they brought him home with deep burns on the lower part of his body. Grandmother made a liniment of Air Slack Lime and linseed oil and eggs. Then, she would soak bandages and just lay them on the burns. I was very small and it seemed this went on for days and it smelled terrible but Dale healed up with hardly any scars.

Another thing I remember she used to put a drop of Harlem Oil in our eyes once a month. It would burn like the dickens but both Dale and I came out with 20-20 vision. When it was in season, she kept carrot sticks for us to snack on to help our vision.

To flush our kidneys, she used cornsilk tea and asparagus. Our urine odor was horrible.

GRANDMOTHER AND SAMMY

Sᴀᴍᴍʏ ᴡᴀs Aᴜɴᴛ Mᴀʙᴇʟ's English bulldog. One morning, as I went out on the deck to finish my coffee and watch the kids cross the street to go to school getting ready for the track meet. Chris, (my granddaughter's) Basset Hound had the best chair on the porch and was reluctant to give it up. It reminded me of the time my Aunt Mable flew back to Pennsylvania to see her son Tom get married. She had left her Sammy dog with Grandma and Grandpa. Sammy had been truly spoiled and true to his nature took the best chair in the house. Grandma had never had a dog in the house before and was pretty upset. I had flown home from Louisiana to stay with the two of them while Aunt Mable was gone as neither of them drove.

I told grandmother of a powder called 'dog off', and she was all for trying it. I got some, sprinkled it in the chair, and Sammy would jump up and try but would not stay, and would jump down again. He had always slept with my Aunt and that bothered Grandmother to have a dog in one of her beds. Grandmother said I can't smell that powder and it looks like the sheets so she sprinkled some in Auntie's bed. When Aunty returned, she couldn't figure out why her Sammy dog didn't love her any more and why he would not sleep with her. To my knowledge, Grandmother or myself never told her what happened while she was gone, but Grandmother would get a sly smile that said, "We really did it didn't we."

AUNT MABEL AT THE OCEAN

My Aunt Mable was as fond of the ocean as I was so, when she was in a traveling mood, she would call me and say, what do you think about us going to Long Beach, CA and visiting our cousins Oran and Bernice Berkey. She knew I would jump at the chance.

The Berkey's had a home on the little island of Naples. Oran was a wonderful woodworker and had taken the house and remodeled it until it was a showplace on the island.

Every time we would come to visit, Bernice would call their daughters Linda and Karen and their families to come listen to Aunty. She was wonderful story teller about the wild-west days when she was a girl. This would go on until late in the evening. The next morning we were all sleeping in, and Aunty was always up at the crack of day. She decided to go down stairs and walk by the oceans edge. Aunty was famous for always getting lost, but this time she thought she could find her way home.

She decided she would stay on just one street by the ocean and she marked her spot where she turned by a patch of Shasta Daisies. She was about half way around the island before she turned back in search of her patch of daisies. She hadn't realized that many people had daisy patches in their yards.

When we were up and drinking coffee, Oran asked where Aunty was. I told him she went for a walk and since it had been a couple of hours I was afraid she had lost her way. Oran and I took off searching and sure enough she was still going back and forth looking for her particular bunch of daisies.

Well what the heck, she tried . . .

THE SOOTY STOVEPIPE

ON SUNDAY MORNING AT the Home Ranch, I was awakened by loud voices. My brother Dale and I had gone to a dance in Bonita the night before, and due to everyone passing the hat after closing time the dance went on till about 3:00 am. Bonita was about 40 miles from the ranch.

We had all intentions of sleeping late, but Grandmother was telling Grandpa in no uncertain terms that he was not doing it right. His reply was, "old lady if you think you can do it any better just try."

I finally got up to see what they were doing and if I could help.

They had taken the pipe out of the old wood stove and the flue and were attempting to put it back and it was truly difficult.

If you've never seen soot before, it is that black powdery stuff that sticks to the inside of a stove pipe. While they were handling that old pipe the soot rained down on them and they were as black as the ace of spades, and I wished I'd had film in my camera, especially that afternoon, after they had their baths, setting out in the sunshine I couldn't help remember how beautiful they looked with their snow white hair and all clean again.

QUEEN ELIZABETH

THE MORNING THE TV was busy with Queen Elizabeth's 50th coronation, it reminded me when I was in high school and staying at the Ranch, Betty Winset boarded with Grandmother. Prince Edward gave up the throne to marry Wallie Simpson and American divorcee. They put the Queen Mother on the throne. It was such a big event, and Grandmother let Betty and I stay up late into the night without a fire in the middle of winter to listen to the radio report on this event. Betty sat on my lap to keep us warm. We were wrapped up with a quilt.

Grandmother was as careful of her radio batteries as she was with her food.

You have to understand that back before television and all that, listening to the family radio was a treat and our form of entertainment.

Betty and I got to listen to Jack Armstrong, and Dale got to listen to Amos and Andy. Grandma and Grandpa listened to the news. Of course the radio never got turned on at any other time to save on batteries.

I wonder how many of the young folks today take the time to listen to the radio—other than when they are in their cars . . .

MOTHER AND THE BISCUITS

My mother was famous throughout the Sulpher Springs Valley for her buttermilk biscuits. One day, Dale came home and said, "'Mother, I have a couple of pretty important friends coming by. Could I invite them for a Sunday dinner?" Her reply was, "what time do you want it." One of the friends, Les Armour, was from a well known meat packing company. The other was his best friend, John Lampey, a pilot during World War Two. Mother had killed a couple of home grown frying chickens prepared with all the trimmings plus a large pan of biscuits. The biscuits just seemed to disappear. She spoke up and said, "Boys, when I came to this country to cook for some cowboys, there was an old saying, if you clean up everything on the table you get to kiss the cook. At my age I'm just wondering if I should get up and make some more biscuits."

Clayton And The Secret Box

Oₙₑ ₘₒᵣₙᵢₙg ₐₛ I was getting Francis Stark ready for the day, a lady I was caring for while her nurse was away, I told Francis a funny incident that happened shortly after my brother Dale had passed away. When his daughter Cathy and grandson Clayton were cleaning out his house, Dale and I had taken care of mother the last few years of her life. I had found a box she had tucked away with her mothers false teeth in it. Not knowing exactly what to do with them, I just added my mother's dentures with them as well as my aunt's when we lost her. When Dale was gone, I made room for the box and tucked it in the back of a drawer. Clayton was the one who was cleaning up this particular drawer and was flabbergasted when he ran into this box. He brought them into his mother and said, "What do we do with these, have another memorial service?"

SMOKEY AND DALE

ONE MORNING IN LAS Cruces, New Mexico, I found I was going to be the only one left babysitting our dog, Smokey. I decided I would just load him up and go to Arizona to see my brother Dale. Smokey was a little apprehensive as this was the first trip alone with me that he had taken. When we got there I told him the particular steps near the sleeping porch was his place until we decided to leave. Then I introduced him to Dale as family and thought everything would be fine. Dale went out that evening to the village card social and when he came stumbling home, a little worse for the wear, that evening, Smokey met him at the gate and refused to let him in so Dale had to hunt up a bed at the neighbors. The next morning he told me about it and said, "If I had a dog I would want him just like Smokey."

Tommy's Times At Cochise

WHEN CGEE, CHRIS, AND Tommy Laney came home to live with Grandmother, Dale and me, in Cochise, Arizona, Tommy was only about three years old. Tommy's Uncle Dale was crazy about him. He was at that cute age, and some of the things he pulled were truly amusing.

One day, Dale had a back hoe come in and dig a deep leach line for the septic tank overflow. Dale was down in the ditch shoveling out a little dirt the back hoe didn't get. Tommy was on top with his little shovel shoveling it back on top of his Uncle Dale. When I came out, Tommy said, "Look Grandma I am helping Uncle Dale."

Another time while they were staying there, I was raising prize Himalayan cats. One day Dale heard Tommy say, "Look Uncle Dale, bearcat bubbles." He had my prize Himalayan, holding her head in our little water bucket.

Another time Dale had poured some compound into the toilet that was supposed to eat the roots out of the septic. The compound resembled little black bee bees. Tommy had been taking a nap, and when he awoke he wandered into the bathroom and let fly. When he looked down and saw the little black balls, he came screaming, "Grandma, Grandma, my pee-pee is broke, come look." After he had shown us what he meant, we all had a good laugh.

MOTHER, THE PAINT
BUCKET AND THE LADDER

THE OTHER DAY, WHILE helping Ruth Shilling in Cochise, Arizona in painting her house, I was reminded of a story of my mother that I relayed to her. Mother and I were busy building and painting her new house in Cochise, and I was delegated to do all the trim and delicate painting. I was painting the front porch ceiling with Forest Green enamel. I was being very careful not to spill a drop. I had moved my ladder to the West corner, very nearly finished, when Mother came out to look over the job. She said, "I just don't see how you do it. If I had been painting I would have paint all over me and the floor. You are doing a super job." With that, she turned back into the house, hooked her toe in my step ladder causing it to collapse, myself and the paint bucket came tumbling down. That is one time I can't brag that I never spilled a drop.

The Old Square Grand Piano

The Pearce Silver Mine was known for being one of the richest mines in Arizona. Mr. Pearce had bought his wife a beautiful square grand piano. When he decided to leave, Grandmother and her daughter Mable traded for the piano.

It was a treasure and Grandmother thought it brought the community together because she would give a big potluck dinner and people would come from miles around to play and sing hymns. It was the nearest thing at that time they had for a church gathering.

When Gale was four, a salesman from Kansas City Music College came through selling correspondence courses to people in the Valley. Gale's mother was working at Riggs's Ranch at the time, and signed up for the course for her daughter. Gale can still remember her mother making her practice, and by the time she was nine, she was into concert music and only had 22 more lessons to graduate from the Music College. This is when her mother decided to make the move to the White Mountains with Pecos. Needless to say, there was not a piano in her future up there, and she forgot most of what she learned.

When she moved back, her Grandmother gave her lessons from a Mrs. Ewing at Pearce who taught quite differently than the correspondence course. When Gale was in high school they formed a school band. She was now playing 'swing' music mostly by ear.

The old square grand piano was the center of attraction at the ranch until her Aunt Mable started a dance hall down in Douglas, Arizona where she took the old piano. When the dance closed, it went to Gales's father's house in Douglas where it remained for several years. When Gale remarried, she and Buck went to live at the old ranch. They also rescued the old piano and moved it to its original spot. Its sad end started when Pug and Bill Scott were afraid the old ranch house might burn down after Gale and Buck left, and they took the piano to Bill's shop. Pug wanted to restore it but it was going to be quite expensive because they had to send to England for replacement parts. During this time, Bill got throat cancer and they had to sell their shop to David Miller. He needed room for other equipment, so he let our other neighbor; Paul Riggs take it and store it in his old classic car barn.

Paul said he did not know the piano belonged to Gale and when Lee Burnett came up a junk dealer, he sold it to him to get more room for his cars. Lee took it home with the idea of peddling the ivory keys and brass sounding board. When Gale found out what had happened, she had been away for a couple of years. She asked Lee for the piano back but it had been rained on and the beautiful wood was ruined and Lee wasn't sure he had all the parts. It was a sad end for such a beautiful instrument.

DITCH DAY

ON OUR HIGH SCHOOL ditch day, our teacher, Mike Maffeo had a new car and since there were only five in our class, we all crowded in. He took us to Tucson and we all went to an orphanage, then had lunch, and then went out through Colossal Cave. From there, we went to Tombstone. We ended up at the Crystal Palace, it was evening by this time and our sight- seeing and travels were ending. Our teacher ordered us all fancy non-alcoholic cokes. We were dancing, having so much fun cutting up we didn't need booze. The old town marshal had been keeping a close eye on us and when he walked over to our table we thought we were in trouble. He looked at me directly and asked, "Little girl, may I ask your name?" I told him and he said, "Would your mother's name be Bernice Rathbun?" I replied, "It used to be," and he said, "Little girl, I used to date your mother before you were a twinkle in her eye." His name was Chesley Miller.

Buck 'Crashed' Our Hen Party

ONE DAY WHEN MOTHER and I were living in my mobile home in Tucson, I had invited a few of her friends over for ice cream and cake; sort of a hens party. Buck, who was very fond of my mother had the opportunity to stop by. He had two girl friends with him. Mother was setting on the couch with the sun shining in the window behind her. Buck sat beside her and she looked up at him with his new haircut she said, "Buck, is your hair as white as it looks to me or is it all gone?" She wasn't able to see very well at this time, and Buck had to change the subject when we all had laughed. He walked to the piano where I had pictures. He picked up one and told his girlfriend, "This is my sweet little daughter CGee." Then he said, "This is my wife when she was young and beautiful."

Buck had been blind or a few weeks, and I had fired back at him, "Buck I am still young and beautiful, are you having eye problems again?" His return, "Yeh, but you have put on little lard since you and I were together." "Yes," I said, "You kept me pretty well starved down." Buck replied with, "Little girl if you ever want to get your figure back just give me a call." After they left, the girls all said, "He was so wonderful, how could you let him go?" I never met but one person who wasn't enchanted by him. He had made a pass at her when he was drunk and she never forgave him. To his dying day, I think he loved my mother best of all. Drunk or sober, he was right there whcn there was something that needed doing, and he loved to watch her paint. CGee always proudly called him daddy even though at times she could get very angry at him, but he made our lives interesting for about 9 ½ years.

CLOVERDALE PICNIC

CLOVERDALE PICNIC WAS SORT of a highlight of the year. Since Buck was from New Mexico it was a must for him as well as for the old pioneer Cowboys Picnic was for Gale. A group of good friends got together and decided to go to Cloverdale, about150 miles from the ranch. You planned on going early and planned on not coming back until the sun came up. It was such a popular event they had to put in a landing strip for people who would fly in. There would be a big bbq beef dinner, horseshoes, card games, all kinds of activities for the kids and dance all night to the music of Forrest Delk.

Pug and Bill Scott flew into the picnic. Liz and Kenneth Gunner drove as did Buck, Gale, CGee, and Sonny. Of course Cloverdale being about 50 miles from the nearest store, everyone brought their own refreshments. There was a coffee pot on the fire all the time.

Kenneth Gunner, if I hadn't told you in another story was quite a drinking cowboy. Elizabeth would seldom go to these affairs as he was a little much. He was generally known as opening up his bottle and throwing the cork away as he didn't intend to stop until it was gone.

Pug, Kenneth's sister, had brought a case of Jack Daniels. Needless to say, Buck and Kenny made them a helping hand to dispense with their supply. This particular evening, Elizabeth had been the best sport I had ever seen, and seemed to be having a real good time until she jumped up, caught a tree limb and was swinging back and forth. Kenny looked up and saw her, just bulldogged her and knocking the breath out of her, and the party was over for the evening. We just rolled her up in her bed, made her comfortable and went right on dancing until the sun came up.

Time to go home; of course Gale had to drive. When they arrived at the ranch, they found they had company. Buck's sister and family from California (Vivian) whom Gale had never met were waiting to visit with them. Buck, CGee and Sonny said hello and went to bed. Gale who hadn't had any sleep had to entertain them and cook a big dinner for them.

Another Cloverdale picnic that Buck and Gale went to; her mother had made them an angel food cake. Gale had been on an ulcer diet and ran out of milk.

Buck told her they would go by the Grey ranch, they would have milk. Sure enough they probably had milk but there was no one home. Buck said we would go to Animas, they have a store there. This being Sunday, it was closed. Buck said, I know Hatchita will have milk, but with the same results. However, Buck found a little friend, Pete English with a Jim Beam jug, setting on the steps of one of the saloons waiting for it to open.

Buck joined him and Gale brought out the angle food cake. He and Pete had cake and Jim Beam. Buck said, "My sister Phoebe lives in Columbus, NM its only about 30 miles to the border and she will have milk."

When they got there, they found Phoebe had half a can of milk so they saddled up, went into Mexico and partied until they had to come back. Going home to Arizona they had to go through Deming and they stopped at Pine Lodge where they were able to get a quart of milk. Come Monday morning just in time for Gale to warm up her school bus and get on the road. Now families wonder why she wants to sleep in when she gets the chance.

GRANDMAS ALMOST
BOYFRIEND

THIS MORNING BROUGHT TO mind a story of how CGee managed to get rid of one of her mother's boyfriends. The neighbors in Las Cruces gave Gale a set of bed rails which she had been looking for quite a long time. She had two old fashioned headboards, and it seems one of Gales old friends came to take her out to dinner. She had been out helping CGee` put up some fence. Gale's friend, being an old time cowboy, made a suggestion to make it easier for CGee. So Gale took off to go clean up to go out. CGee had the old guy helping her. He thought CGee would quit when she ran out of stays, but she walked over and got her mother's bed rails and went on with the fence. By this time it was nearly too dark to work and he thought they would surly have to stop.

CGee ran, got her pickup and shined her lights on the fence line so they could finish up. Needless to say, he didn't invite Gale out to dinner again. CGee said, "I'll bet he never tells anyone else they are doing it all wrong or try's to show them how it's done."

THE MISSING BODY

MY FRIEND, BETTY GWEN, told me on the phone the other day, if my book didn't include my Aunt's favorite story which she had won prizes for, it would not be complete.

The strange thing about this phone call, was that my Aunt had passed away before the last story was ever written . . .

Aunt Mabel's husband, Mart, as I have mentioned earlier in the book, was quite a drinker. Back in the "boot leg" days Aunt Mabel thought there were a lot of things more important things to spend their money on than boot leg booze. She told Uncle Mart that if he didn't give it up, she was going to take their baby, Tom, and leave him. It was agreed, that he would go down to Douglas and take the "cure" now called drying out cold turkey.

When he returned home he was an ideal husband. My Aunt was very much in love and proud of him. After a period of time, Uncle Mart got a message that an old friend and prospector up in the Courtland area had died. His family asked Mart to come up to Courtland, and clean up the body and get him dressed and into a home-made Coffin. Then get him to Gleason for the funeral.

Uncle Mart said that since this happened in the summer time, and the old man had been dead about a week, he was pretty ripe. He said the odor was so bad that he didn't think he could get him ready. He looked up a friend who knew the local boot legger to get a jug or two. After fortifying themselves, they cleaned up the body, got it dress and into the coffin. Then they loaded the coffin into the back of an old wooden wagon.

Now for those of you not familiar with that area, it was full of little rolling hills. The road were little more than cow paths. Anyway, the boys set off with the old man and finished off their jugs as they went bouncing along the cow path. When they arrived in Gleason where everyone was waiting for the funeral, they discovered they had lost the coffin . . .

Now the part of my Aunt's story she did not live to hear was told by Chris, her Great Niece.

Chris, my granddaughter, was working on the road in an adjoining state **three** generations later. A couple of boys were car pooling with her, and one was telling a story. He said his wife told him the wildest story. She said her mother told her that her grand father had died and that some crazy drunken cowboy had lost him on the way to the funeral. My Grand daughter asked the boy if he would like the rest of the story? They looked at her like she was nuts and she told them that that drunken cowboy was her Great Uncle Mart . . .

Pecos Higgins

Tʜᴇ ꜰᴏʟʟᴏᴡɪɴɢ sᴛᴏʀʏ ᴀʙᴏᴜᴛ Calico and the Poems were written by Pecos Higgins especially for Gale C. Ginn. Pecos was Gale's Step Dad and they enjoyed a special relationship.

Gale   Pecos   CGee

The following Calico text is as originally written with no changes . . .

"Dear Gale, This is about all I can write about our old friend, Calico. So you can finish it up after he come into you life in 1931 or '32.' He was five years old in 1921. You can figure up how old he was when he died. This story and poem are not as good as he was, but the best that I can do. I never expect to ride another one like him. I am thanking the prison officers for letting me send this to you . . ."

As ever, Pecos

THE STORY OF CALICO

ON THE SOUTH WESTERN slope of old Mt. Baldy, in the late fall of 1920, with a bad snow storm falling, I am sure was the first time that any man ever laid eyes on a pretty Paint pony, that was four years old at the time and in the company of two other little maverick studs of about his age and one sorrel branded gelding several years older. They were drifting south from the storm and to get to lower country, for the animal's instinct told them the snow storm was going to be a bad one and it was.

For we never saw the ground in them parts any more that whole darn winter.

I was very busy that day trying to get the outfit's cattle that I worked for, to the country about 20 miles from there, where the snow did not get so deep and plenty of oak brush for them to eat all winter...

Being alone, and not having any time to handle any ponies then, I just looked at the Paint as they run off and said, "Little fellow, I'll own you some day."

All winter, after I got the cattle down, I would think of my Paint pony high up on the head of Rock Creek in the deep snow. They could not get any lower down on account of the drift fence that cut them off. I was glad of that, for thar *(there)* was people lower down and they might have caught him before I seen him again. He was a maverick and belonged to the cowboy that caught him. He lived in a big wild country where only a few trappers and cowboys ever went.

When winter was over, we moved the cattle up thare again for the summer and I staid *(stayed)* with them. Every day when I was riding, I had my eye out for that Paint pony. Thare was lots of herds of Wild horses, but very hard to see in the thick timber. It was getting late in the summer of 1921 and I had been looking for my pony since early spring. Most every day I rode in the country where he was likely to be. I began to think that someone had beat me to him, until one day I rode up on a horse that had been shot and killed. So I got down to look him over and found he was one of the ponies that was with the Paint when I seen them the fall before.

I took the trail where they had been running and did not go far until I found another one. Not so far from him, the branded gelding lay. One track went on – the ponies had been killed the day before. I followed the one track as far as I could, for I knew it must be the Pinto and someone was trying to catch him. I lost his track and it was getting late, so I went to camp 10 miles away, trying to figure out why the other ponies were shot if they wanted to get the Pinto. I finally decided that who ever it was did not know too much about wild ponies and figured if they shot all his running mates, he would take up with some old gentle mare that could be handled. Well, they had another guess coming, because thare was no old gentle mares in those parts, tho *(though)* thare was lots of mares and old ones.

Well, I felt pretty good the Pinto was still thare I nearly knew. If I ever saw him again, I would quit whatever I was doing and get after him, no difference if I had started for the doctor or to get married. I had to have that pony!

Time went on and fall of the year was getting near again. It would be no time until I would have to get the old cows together and go with them to the winter range. On day another cowboy come to my camp to stay with me for a few days and get a few cows of his that were mixed with ours.

The next day we rode out to hunt cows, not thinking anything about wild ponies. We had found one or two of his cows and stopped on a high ridge. I staid with them until he went down a very steep trail in the canyon to where thare was water to look for more cows. He had not been long when I heard stock running, rocks rolling and brush a popping.

I cinched up my saddle tighter on Cricket, the pony I was riding, and a good one too – long winded and could run all day. The way he was acting, I knew it was horses coming; even tho I could not see them. I could tell by the noise thare was quite a bunch.

When they come up in sight, thare was my Pinto in the lead, running like a rabbit and jumping logs, rocks and bushes. It looked like he was turning sideways once in a while to keep from flying. The other horses, about ten head, were right on his heels.

When they topped the canyon, they turned down grade, and a lot of down, as we were high up to start with. The only way to stay in sight of them ponies was to get behind them and stay as near to the one in the rear of the bunch as possible. The pines and underbrush was very thick, lots of downed timber and boulders.

The race was on and lasted from about 9:00 am until about 2:00 pm and covered lots of miles. The ponies run because they was wild and scared. They had never seen a horse running with a man on his back before. The other cowboy, Neil Ryan by name, come back to where he left me with the cows. I was gone and the cows were gone. But he struck my trail after them horses and come on as fast as he could; tho it was three or more hours before he found me. By the time he got to me, I had them wild ponies in my pile. Thare little bare feet was getting tender and that fast running was getting old to them. Cricket was shod and good all around and used to running and knew as well as I did that the little soft horses was getting tired. I was in the lead of them and could hold them once in a while. They would trot around and snort.

I was sizing that Pinto up every time he stopped long enough. I only had four head by this time, two mavericks and two branded horses. One of the branded ones had been broke. We was then near my camp and Ryan went for the bunch of gentle horses to put with the wild ones. This being done, I took the lead and we took them to the corral. Going in, the pinto still wanted to lead the bunch and would trot right up behind my horse. He looked more like a striped cloth than anything

I could think of. So I named him Calico before we got to the corral.

It was not long then until I had him roped and a hackamore on him. He was very small, but well made and his teeth showed him to be five years old. He had plenty of sense from the start. Wild as he was, he never fought the rope. In two days time he would eat grain and sugar out of my hand, but sure did not like to be rode and would buck very wicked for a small horse. I kept him staked around my camp and rode him every day or night. Sometimes it was when I got to camp.

When I moved down to the ranch with the stock for winter, Calico would be drove with the other horses, gentle as any of them. That winter was the first time in his five years of life that he ever saw anything for a horse to eat but deep snow drifts and what little grain he could paw down to in the snow on the old White Mountains, in the north eastern part of Arizona.

I had him a good warm stall onto the hay barn and cut a hole so he could eat any time of the day or night, and then come out in the big corral when he liked. He sure was scared of that outfit at first. But, he liked the new hay and would go in and get a bite, then run outside to eat it. The winter being long thare and not so much to do, I was alone, so I put in lots of time training Calico to do every that a cow pony has to do and do it right. With plenty of hay and grains and a little use, he began to grow and get stronger. His bones and muscles grew big for a pony his size. I only took him on short rides and he never knew what a hard days ride was until after he was ten years old.

He growed up to that age and was still a small horse, but just like a chunk of iron and would o until he dropped with no whip or spurs – one of the most wonderful little horses that ever marked Arizona dirt. O course, nobody ever knew what kind of blood was in his veins, but he was supposed to be just a common Indian pony. Them kind of ponies run by the hundreds in that country at the time. No one ever saw one like Calico. His sense actions and color showed that some strain of good blood was in him. He had two different spots on him that was in his skin, not his hair. They were blue and black and could not be seen, only when he was near you. His color was sorrel and white with plenty of class and uniform. The inside of his thighs was speckled with blue spots and one blue spot on the cover of his mouth. On his right muscle of his foreleg, was round black spot a little larger than a silver dollar and a smaller one over his right eye. They was in his hide. The hair that growed thru them was sorrel.

Probably a long time ago, some of Calico and his folk were desert Arabians. He rode and acted like a horse that would weigh one thousand pound or more, tho it would crowd him, at his best, to weigh eight hundred. He growed three hundred of that after he was five years old. He always wanted to be in the lead, his well shaped little head high and short ears perked up. Nothing missed being seen by him where he was being rode or loose. He was what cowboys can an all around pony – good a running wild horses, cutting cattle from round-up, roping and kind of stock, and fair good on the road. H was known, too, as a one man's horse. He did not like strangers. He would do anything for me, because he thought he had to.

Gale Higgins and Cuss Word was the only to persons I ever saw that I really thought he liked. But I think he had quite a bit of love for them two girls. He was seventeen years old when Gale first rode him and eighteen when he first met Cuss, but still acted like he was about six. He had very few different riders and none but me, until after he was fifteen years old.

CALICO'S POEM

In the old White mountains, all covered with snow,
I caught a paint pony, I called Calico.

He was molded just perfect from his head to his toes,
And spotted all over from his tail to his nose.

I broke him to ride, and learned him to rein.
He was quick like a cat and smooth like a plane.

When a stranger came near him, he got pretty wild,
The ones that he knew, he was as safe as a child.

He was good on the range, no matter how rough,
At catching wild cattle that were salty and tough.

And running wild horses, he liked that the best,
Just sit up and ride, and he would do the rest.

He was not real big, but gee was he loud,
As pretty as a picture and stepped real proud.

He had three colors, that dressed him just right,
He was good in the daytime and better at night.

He lived his life in his good old days,
And was rode by people who savvied his ways.

He stayed real fat until the day that he died,
And crossed over the range to the other side,
Where Preachers say everything is fine,
and all spirits meet there in time.

Where grass is green and fine rivers flow,
That will be the place for Calico.

Pecos, Age 72

The following Poems were written by Pecos Higgins' for his book "My Two Sweethearts: Horses and Whiskey" with a Copyright of

© 2004 provided by Gale C. Ginn.

Pecos and Buck discussin' the finer points of whiskey

"I have never started anything that did not turn out a failure, and I started quite a few things, some fights. So I have lots of failures."

"If this book is a failure I am going to change my name, and look for a place where I am not known. Just now I cannot think of where that would be, unless it would be heaven, and I would most likely make another failure trying to get there."

"Moving on to my poems—one day I just got me a stub of a pencil, a piece of wrapping paper, and settled down to writing a verse or two."

"Maybe it don't match up to some of the verses you have read, and I don't expect it to. All the same, at the time it was wrote, I was bawling like a sick calf and pouring my heart and soul into every word and this is it:"

MY Dear Irish Queen

I'm just a poor broke cowboy
In a strange town all alone.
I thought for a while it was Heaven
An' that you were my very own.

I gave to you my heart and soul;
You gave me your love too.
We promised each other undyin' love
Like sweethearts oughta do.

But now you busted my poor heat;
Please change your mind, my Queen,
And I will be the happiest man
That you have ever seen.

I will give you all my money,
My blue hoss and saddle, too.
Listen to me please, sweetheart,
'Cause I'm in love with you.
Your Pecos

My Name is Pecos Higgins

I have punched cows now for years.
Rode herds of leaping ponies,
And necked up many steers,
I was raised in the State of Texas,
Where men were tough and bad.
I never had the schooling,
Like other children had.

I worked for many outfits,
Stood plenty hard old guard.
I have run a livery stable,
And labored long and hard.
I have tried my hand at farming,
And been a Bucher too.
Bootlegged a little whiskey,
And mad a lot of brew.

I have crossed the briney ocean,
With bright lights flashing like stars.
Made love to several maidens,
And drank from many bars.
I have slept down in jungles,
Where bear and panther grew.
All so in perfumed feathers,
With blondes and brunetts too.

Thare is nothing gained by quitting,
I learned that long ago.
Just stay right with the riggin',
If you want to make a show.
I have all ways tried to make it,
Most of the time the cards run wrong.
But I went right on whistling,
Or singing a cowboy song.
If I can float my outfit
Tho times are not so fine.
I will forget about my troubles,
And tip my ht to time.
How I have quit my roaming,
And settled down for keeps.
Altho I am often working,
While other people sleep.

My hens the are a-laying,
And my ponies good and fat.
With steaks and eggs for breakfast,
I will never starve at that.
My home is lonesome,
I need a Maude or Blanche.
Or some other good old cow girl,
On this 7HF Bar Ranch.

"Having nothing else to do between naps, I decided I'd sorta write down a few memories I had of the past. I've still got a few of my verses I wrote on one of my trips. Nothing of special interest happened on that trip, so, with the reader's permission, I'll stick a couple of verses I managed to write on that trip. If you're a hoss lover, you'll enjoy the verse I've wrote concerning a little ole brush-tailed hoss I called Barney. So here goes."

BARNEY

He was just a Spanish pony that roamed the rocky peaks –
He fed upon the mesas and watered from the creeks.
He was known among the cowboys as the kind they'd like to ride
For he savvied every wild cow's tricks, on flats or
mountainsides.
When the bushes went to popin' and the dust began to boil
And the Malapies went to rollin', old Barney quit the soil.
He would bow his neck so proudly;
you could almost hear him say,
"Just pitch slack, ole cowboy, and they'll never get away."

His ears would begin to working and his eyes began to shine
And he seemed to be in glory when I reached down for my line.
When you loosened on his bridle and slacked old Barney's rein
He took out like a bat from hell, speeding like a train.
The way he cut 'round boulders was a mystery to us all –
For, just once in his chases, did old Barney ever fall.
That time he couldn't help it, he bogged down in some springs
While trying to catch a maverick that had
swapped his legs for wings.

W caught him up one summer, the grass was green and tall,
He looked just like a picture, hung on some hoss lover's wall.
His hair was soft and silky and a crease was down his back
He looked just like a race horse from a Tia Juana tack.
One morning after reaching camp, it was
along 'bout half past three

He started rolling and a-groaning, as a sick hoss could be.
I gave him care and treatment down by my river's side
But I guess the good Lord needed him, for poor Barney died.

Now when we wrangle horses out in the wild cow land
There's a little bay that's missing, he wore the Spanish brand.
It's hard to do without him and to remember he died,
But he's gone to help the cowboys that have
crossed the great divide.
I don't know how the "waddies" work up in the Lord's cow land
But I'll lay great odds to one that old Barney makes a hand.
And I'm hoping that when my time comes to
cross the great divide
I will always call for Barney – should I want to take a ride.

Yes folks, ole Barney was all hoss, God love his old hide! Having written of him sorta makes me want to add another poem because this bit of "Hell on the Mountain" I write of was a-straddle ole Barney. If you are an ole cow han', you'll savy the mountain picture I try to paint with words. If you are a dude, just bear this verse in mind the next time you leave a hotel or camp and head for the mountains. Once up there, you'll appreciate this poem I call –

HELL ON THE MOUNTAIN

It was far upon the mountain among the lonesome pines
Where the Aspen grow thick as hell – so goes the wild grape
vines
You hunt you saddle horses thru canyons, dales and dells
Strain your eyes looking for tracks – your ears, listening for
bells.
Cow punching was once a pleasure – working with top hands
With damn good mounts beneath that almost knew the bran.
But don't never get by your lonesome, cause the wise cows
understand
And they head right for the bushes and the rocky, broken land.

There's been lots of changes since I came upon this world's soil
But a cowboy still has hardships – loneliness and toil.
Smart cows can get the best of you up where the woodbine twine
And there's not so many cowboys can rope on in the pine.
There's cowboys around the cities that wear real fancy clothes,
That would swap them for a G-string if they knew the
cowboys woes.
If it was up to them to gather stock out of friar-brush 'n leaf,
This country would be out of luck – and damn well out of beef.

Last night, layin' in my suggan, that is neither soft or warm,
Dressed in Levis and shirt that had never known an ion,
I heard from a big ole pine tree the hooting of an owl,
While from a canyon, far below, came a lobo's mournful howl.
I fell asleep, I recon, 'cause it sorta seems to me

I was dancing with some maidens fair, as pretty as could be.
Then it seems I rode a bony and roped Billy the kid,
Then square-danced with all the gals until the sun was hid.

When I woke up by my lonesome, it was raining Billy hell,
'N thundering so loud that I couldn't hear myself yell.
Old barney was a –snorting with his tail turned into the wind
My suggan blowed all to hell, I guess- I never seen it again.
But that's life on a mountain – how cowboys earn their pay
And considers himself lucky to earn one buck a day.
So when you see some city cowboy a'braggin' and a shouting
Just ask him if he's ever spent a night of "Hell on the
Mountain."

How I Growed Up

I been on the range about 75 years,
A handling cows, Broncos and steers.
I have thought to myself, when I was alone,
The cowboys I would have, if an outfit I'd own.
Every Puncher I'd work, would be just right,
An could tell a cow's though, when she came into sight.
And no cow job would he ever shirk,
If the spread was mine, that's the kind I'd work.

He could ride any Bronco,
No difference how bad.
And has rustled them long ears,
Since he was a lad. And stood many guards,
In the days of stampedes,
Punched cows on the Baldy's, Jungles and Weeds.
And no cow job would he ever shirk,
If the spread was mine, that's the kind I'd work.

But time they say, many changes bring,
A lot I have learned, right here in this spring.
That the less you know, and I allow as how,
They are writing books, how to punch cows . . .

PRISON

I landed in this prison camp, Sept 10th, I believe,
And I figured it was pretty tough and I would have to leave.
I stood around a day or two keeping out of people's way,
And sized things up here all about, then decided I'd better stay.
I put my head to workin', that is made of solid bone,
And found that there are plenty of things we do not have at home.
When the boss man spoke, their words were kind, that seemed
to me so strange,
For the toughest boss-men this side of hell,
Are the ones that ride the range.

The house-keepers and cooks at our house I will say are few,
Whenever we eat we have to cook and furnish the groceries too.
The water we use we carry from the creek,
the wood we chop it down,
We have to have money to pay for the
chuck whenever we go to town.
Our laundry we do with a tub and a board,
it never is very clean,
And the baths are put off "cuz" the water
is cold, we don't ever have any steam.
Our beds they are wet with pack mule's sweat, when it's carried
into camp in the nite,
And I kick it straight away after dark,
as there is not a chance for a light.

Now old Uncle Sam, is a fine old man, the way it seems to me,

His eats and beds and his shower-baths,
tobacco, and clothes all free.
A man who would ask for anything
more would surely have his nerve,
He should be thrown in the Tucson
jail with a hundred years to serve.
So we will forget how hard we were
hit when we hocked this little jam,
But we will always remember Old '43
and Xmas with Uncle Sam.
My hat is off to the Prison Boss and the year of '43,
But the sooner I get where the cow-ponies live,
the better it will be.

I Dreamed I Was Riding A Pony

I dreamed I was riding a pony, as perfect as Nature could mold,
His mane was the color of silver, his body the color of gold.
His eye was the same as an eagle; his step was just like a deer,
And the rigging I had all fit him, I'll try to describe it here

The bit was made by Kelly, with the shanks al silver inlaid,
The headstall and reins came from Dwyres,
     the best that was ever made.
The saddle was made by N. Porter, the nicest the West ever saw,
The blanket the most brilliant colors ever
     wove by a Navajo squaw.

And sir, when I mounted this pony, his like I will say is few,
I had to be togged just like him or else I would not do.
My hat was 5X Beaver, John Stetson the brand,
My handkerchief from the Stockman's store, in a Colorado land.
My shirt it come from Montgomery, made of silk loud and stout,
My pants wore the trademark of Levi,
     the best that ever come out.
Sears and Roebuck was the people that handled
     the gloves that I wore,
My chaps was made by Sietzler, there was
     never one like them before.

My boots they come from Justin Spurs made by J.O. Bass,

Should anyone seen the outfit, thair thought
would have been class.
The country was rich with color, as we skipped along the trail,
From the Buckhorn ranch to Pine Top, where Pecos gets his mail.
The trail is a little winding, thru bushes and some thorns,
And many time I have rode it, to read the Hoofs & Horns.
After seeing the Tucson rodeo, the best that I ever have seen,
I come back to the White Mountains; this
poem came along in a dream.

Friends, the old train is still chugging towards Fort Worth according to the verses before me. I wonder if I couldn't slip in a couple of short ones that an ole friend of mine give me. His poetical efforts runs a little different than mine, but he paints you a word picture that you can just naturally see when you start reading it. If you have ever seen a deserted mining town, you will agree with me that Cotton, that's my buddy's name, knows what he's writing about. So, here tis!

GHOST CITY

Surrounded by snow-capped mountains
In a valley silent and quiet,
Stands a city now long deserted
That once was gay and bright.
A city which like a desert flower
Sprung overnight from the sand,
A Mecca for miners and ranchers
And homesteaders seeking new land.
Silent witness of many a shooting fray
And stories of new-found gold,
Oh! Could it but echo the laughter 'n such?
That filled it in the days of old.
T'would carry you back four score or more
To the birth of the Golden West
When men and women, both good and bad,
From its soil were seeking to wrest
The precious metals they hungered for,
Following always the call of Gold,
From cities, states and distant lands,
Adventurous both young and old.
Came to this city, once bright n' gay,
Now braving the desert's blast
Of howling sand and blistering sun
Just a ghost from out of the past.

Well now, I recon if you can't just see a picture of some old western town after reading that "Ghost City" verse, you haven't been out west. Nor is your imagination working on all cylinders if his "Desert Dusk" can't jerk you out of that comfortable chair you're no doubt sitting in and put you out on the desert with Cotton's true description of a typical Arizona sunset. I've seen hundreds of these beautiful paintings of nature, (to steal a phrase from the verse below) and I want you to enjoy this one even though you are seated in some room miles and miles away from the desert.

DESERT DUSK

Dusk draws near – the golden sun
Sinks slowly into its mold
Of snow-capped distant mountains
Like a ball of burnished gold.
Night birds call to absent mates
From cacti, towering and high
As nature paints with a thousand hues
A beautiful sunset sky.
Silence prevails, but for tumblin' weeds
Bouncing around over the ground,
Propelled by brisk, playful zephyrs
That dance gaily all around.
Then comes the dusk with cloaks of dark
First grey, then darkest blues,
To enshroud this painting of nature,
This sky of a thousand hues.
Why, thought I, as I gazed above,
At the slowly darkening sky,
Must beautiful things be eventually dark-?
Even as you and I?

. . .

In 2005, some friends of mine, Don & Betty Minden, drove us all over to the Cowboy Picnic down at Turkey Creek in Southern Arizona. We had fun re-exploring some of the places in the above stories. For me, it was a time for a lot of memories to boil up from my life. Naturally, being the quite, reserved person that you all know, I had to relate some of these memories with my old cowboy and cowgirl friends at the picnic.

In the following photograph I'm passing on one the poems I had memorized from Pecos' story telling times. They gave me an award for talking the longest and telling the best poem they had ever heard.

Ya all take care now, ya hear?

Gale entertaining folks with Poems at the Southeastern Arizona Pioneer Cowboy Picnic held at Turkey Creek, Arizona in 2005.

She told one of Pecos' poems for about 20 minutes

and won the Picnic prize for story telling.

This wraps up my story telling for the "book." If I ever have the time to continue, or add to this narration, I would have to tell you all the funny stories in my life as it **really** happened . . .

THE END

GLOSSARY OF WESTERN TERMS

Page	Sic No.	Term	Meaning
25	1	chuck	A cowboy's breakfast, lunch or dinner
31	2	dry land field	This is putting in a crop and praying for rain
32	3	casement	This is the bottom of a window frame
32	4	rootin-tootin	A hell raising party
39	5	catch-rope	Lariat
39	6	flat	A flat, empty spot among rolling land
41	7	circingle	This is a modified cinch with handles on top rather than a saddle
41	8	ramuda	A ranch or cowboys string of horses
42	9	earing	Holding a horse by its ears for control
42	10	snubbed	Tie a horse up close so it can't move
45	11	stockman	Took care of all the livestock
58	12	Bull Durham	Roll your own cigarettes

58	13	Prince Albert, Velvet	Tins of tobacco
59	14	Rocky Mt. Oysters	Bull's testical nuts
59	15	High Yellow	A mixed Negro & Anglo blood
64	16	catclaw	A desert plant that has curved spines shaped like a cat's claw
67	17	cowboyed	Slang for the work cowboys perform